Sources for THE NEW ENGLAND MIND:
THE SEVENTEENTH CENTURY

Sources for
The New England Mind:
The Seventeenth Century

By Perry Miller

Edited by James Hoopes

The Institute of Early American History and Culture
Williamsburg, Virginia

*The Institute of Early American History and Culture
is sponsored jointly by The College of William and Mary
and The Colonial Williamsburg Foundation.*

Contents

Introduction

AMONG American historians active in the last one hundred years only two, Charles Beard and Frederick Jackson Turner, surpass Perry Miller in influence, though his intellectual achievements were arguably superior even to theirs. As with their most important writings, Miller's greatest work still disturbs the peace. His two-volume *New England Mind* (1939, 1953) is honored by challenge or correction every publishing season, which proves that the book is very much alive. Yet though much subsequent scholarship has built on his, and though students he trained have sometimes become his defenders, Miller did not leave behind a well-defined and easily recognizable school of interpretation in the sense that Beard and Turner did. This contrast is more remarkable still in view of Miller's having succeeded Beard and Turner by, respectively, one and two generations, so there has been less time for erosion of his influence and significance. Perhaps his fate contrasts so sharply with theirs because while those two great historians are identified with the fairly fathomable forces of economy and environment, Miller stands for the more menacing, because more difficult to understand, power of ideas in history.

Ideas were not ominous so long as they were the ordinary, high-sounding abstractions of American history, such as "political and religious freedom." Bancroft, Palfrey, and other nineteenth-century historians who praised their forebears' love of liberty found nothing to fear in Puritan ideas. Neither did Brooks Adams who, though he took the opposite point of view and called the Puritans religious autocrats, thought of them as safely dead. Not until the early twentieth-century polemics of George Santayana, Van Wyck Brooks, and H. L. Mencken was Puritanism reborn as a contemporary menace, but the danger was more emotional than intellectual, with "puritanical" becoming a catch-all label for the repression of personal, sexual, and artistic impulses. That ideas had counted for little or nothing to the Puritans themselves seemed firmly and finally proved in 1921 when James Truslow Adams published *The Founding of New England,* which, like Beard's slightly earlier work on the Constitution, offered a refreshingly realistic approach by insisting on the importance of economic motives.[1]

The supremacy of economic interests over ideas as motives for human action seemed obvious to many who experienced the apparently mindless prosperity of the 1920s and the genuinely stricken economy of the 1930s, but in 1933 one beginning scholar laid himself "open to the charge of being so very naïve as to believe that the way men think has some influence upon their actions." This was in *Orthodoxy in Massachusetts,* Perry Miller's first book. There he argued that the founding of the Massachusetts Bay Colony was not undertaken for economic reasons alone but had also been a crusade for an idea, the idea of individually congregated churches within Anglicanism, or, in short, the idea of non-separating Congregationalism.[2] Miller's emphasis on the historical significance of Puritan ideas was somewhat antedated by the work of his Harvard colleagues Samuel Eliot Morison and Kenneth Murdock,[3] but no one had ever before elaborated so complex and sophisticated a pattern of thought within the Puritan intellect as non-separating Congregationalism. Yet however ingenious the ratiocination that permitted New England Puritans to consider themselves loyal members of the Church of England even at the very moment they were fleeing its hierarchy, *Orthodoxy in Massachusetts,* by the limitation of its subject, could make the Puritans no more than clever pleaders of a special cause. If by leaving England they had acted briefly in behalf of an idea, it seemed an eccentric idea, related neither to the larger world of seventeenth-century thought nor to developments subsequent to the Puritans' arrival in New England. Even Morison's splendid volumes celebrating Harvard's 1936 tercentenary,[4] which showed that New England's first college offered aspiring ministers not cramped sectarianism but rather a liberal arts education as broad as that of any European university of the time, did not indicate that such learning had substantially affected New England history.

The challenge of demonstrating the significance of ideas in Puritan actions was finally met in 1939 by Miller's *The New England Mind: The Seventeenth Century,* which bore a clear relationship to the earlier *Orthodoxy in Massachusetts.* The former book had argued that the Puritans were non-separating Congregationalists, and the latter explored the ideas underlying and justifying their Congregationalism. At the root of the matter was the Puritans' attachment to the view that a properly constituted church was one in which the elect of God recognized each other as such and voluntarily covenanted with each other to form a congregation as cleansed as humanly possible of the unregenerate. This was the idea of church covenant, and Miller attributed it to utopianism, traditional desires to strengthen the communal bond, and contemporaneous political and economic forces that emphasized the importance of the individual will.[5] The Puritans themselves naturally sought more timeless sanctions than these for the constitution of their churches, but they did not have the basis they would have liked most of all: the idea of church covenant unfortunately was not mentioned in the New Testament. Instead, the church covenant's legitimacy was established by ideas, or what Miller called the Puritans' "intellectual heritage."

In the greatest single act of discovery in American historical writing Miller's book revealed that the Puritans had drawn from astonishingly broad and varied ideas to create what seemed to them a perfectly coherent system of thought. That they had relied on previous Protestant theology was of course no surprise; but that they had also shared the new seventeenth-century emphasis on method, been interested in humanism and Classical culture, and based much of their thought on natural philosophy refuted all smug dismissals of Puritanism as narrow, sectarian, and antipathetic to either Renaissance or twentieth-century sensibilities. As if that were not enough, Miller traced the Puritans' intricate interweaving of these ideas into new intellectual creations in "Cosmology," "Anthropology," and "Sociology." He showed the great influence on Puritans of the sixteenth-century logician and educational reformer Peter Ramus, who gave them confidence in the power of the human mind and senses to read God's word as written not only in the Bible but also in the book of nature. From natural philosophy in turn came their understanding of human psychology and thus of the means of conversion, especially the sermon, through which divine grace was effected. From the Old Testament came their notion that God dealt with men in a covenant, from which they took assurance that in grace He voluntarily obliged Himself to give men the strength to walk in the way of righteousness and salvation. And from the covenant of grace, by logic, they thankfully extrapolated what they had been unable to find in the New Testament, the church covenant.

If this massive architecture of ideas that the Puritans constructed out of materials from their intellectual heritage was impressively coherent, it was not easily reconciled with some of their most personal religious convictions. Running through *The New England Mind: The Seventeenth Century* is a tension between the Puritans' intellectual heritage and what I have elsewhere called their three main "pietistical ideas": (1) the universe is governed absolutely by a mysterious force—"God"; (2) since He created the world good and beautiful, depraved man is the source of all disharmony—"sin"; and (3) while fallen man cannot restore harmony, for a few men God performs this saving work—"regeneration." The Puritans had assumed that because God created the world as a unity, there could be no contradiction between these "basic ideas" of their piety and whatever truth resided in their intellectual heritage. Therefore Miller could portray them not only as men of piety but also as friends of new learning, participants in the Renaissance, and unwitting advocates of modernism. But the far more important point, in terms of their own experience, was that "along with the piety there existed in the minds of Puritans many tenets and attitudes that had no inherent connection with it, and some that could be reconciled to it only with difficulty."[6]

In Miller's interpretation the danger of ideas is that they can serve purposes other than those for which they are created. Covenant theory was meant to encourage human action and responsibility while, at the same time, guarding against the heresy that the will is free, that man may achieve salvation by his own efforts. Although Miller knew that theologians before the Puritans had used covenant theory, he believed that the Puritans had given it an extraordinary emphasis and had thus tacitly admitted that "piety was on the wane."[7] Yet the profound irony as he saw it was that though covenant theory was meant to preserve piety it also worked against it. For a covenant was an agreement, and "man's will was engaged to it, not so much out of fear of the Lord as out of respect for his given word" and because of the reasonableness of the bargain that had been struck. The Puritan theorists had made themselves hostages of their intellectual heritage and of the rising spirit of their age, which was devaluing arbitrary authority in favor of voluntary contractualism as the basis of social as well as spiritual relationships. The Puritans' covenant theory lent strength to "explicit rationalism and constitutionalism," so that "they were foredoomed to the exciting but hopeless task of stabilizing it along with their inherited belief in unilateral authority and divine revelation."[8]

Miller was not an intellectual determinist in the sense that he believed ideas alone were important, but he was convinced that whatever order or coherence existed in human history had been supplied by the human mind. Ideas were not the only historical determinants, but social history, he argued, could not be satisfactorily understood without reference to minds that had experienced it. For those minds had not only experienced social change, they had also responded to it, and their response helped to determine succeeding developments in society as well as in thought. Even though the Puritans perhaps took up covenant theory "not so much for theological as for social and economic reasons," they could not escape the consequences of their intellectual failure, their inability to reconcile human freedom with divine authority. Therefore, "implicit in these latent antagonisms" lay the future history of New England, which "might be most succinctly described as a progressive disintegration of the federal [i.e., covenant] theology."[9]

Approaching social and political history through its relation to covenant theory was the strategy of Miller's second volume, *The New England Mind: From Colony to Province* (1953). Ranging from events as spectacular as the Salem witch trials to matters as mundane as the inadequate supply of specie, he charted the gradual discrediting of covenant theory as a basis for established Congregationalism. Yet the power of ideas was not discredited, for as the orthodox strove to fend off secularism and a society founded on voluntary agreements rather than feudal obligations, they began to apply the covenant to the whole society, to sinners as well as to saints. This tactic failed as a lever of social control, but it created the myth of national covenant, of a special relation between God and New England (later America), which would have a large, albeit difficult to measure, impact on subsequent history. And even the death of covenant theory was in a sense a victory for ideas, that is for pietistical ideas and the awful power of an uncovenanted God. By ending his book with a glimpse of young Jonathan Edwards on his way to Boston to preach on the greatness of man's dependence on God, Miller pointed forward to the principal social event of the eighteenth century, the Great Awakening and a revival of Puritan purpose.

Recognition of the magnificence of Miller's accomplishment came in many ways. Perhaps most eloquent was the tribute paid by his student Edmund Morgan shortly after Miller's death in 1963, that not until "historians become philosophers and philosophers historians will the full significance of his achievement be understood."[10] David Hollinger has splendidly stated that Miller's work rose to the level of art, not only because he wrote "with resonance and verbal richness, but because his organization, architecture, and intricacy of conception reveal an intensely purposive and creative activity."[11] Yet even the vast quantity of direct praise is surpassed in significance by the astonishing amount of scholarly energy devoted to American Puritanism since Miller's day. Rather than being played out, as one of Miller's professors had discouragingly told him when he was a graduate student, Puritan New England, since the publication of *The New England Mind,* has become one of the richest veins in American history. Most of this work, whether it has challenged or supported Miller, would never have been done without his pioneering volumes. Yet *The New England Mind* towers over the great mass of this subsequent scholarship, and in the view of some of the best contemporary scholars, such as David Hall, remains after forty years our single best work on American Puritanism.[12] And in other fields there is no book to rival it; *The New England Mind* is the masterwork of twentieth-century American historiography.

The New England Mind is distinguished from later scholarship by the same characteristic that separated it from preceding work, namely Miller's amazing range and comprehensiveness, which enabled him to relate theological ideas, natural philosophy, and literary form to society, economics, and politics. Since Miller's time Puritanism has for the most part been subdivided into various specialized preserves, some focusing on social history, some on ideas, and some on rhetoric and other literary questions. This narrowing of focus has engendered work of great intensity, and many inadequacies in *The New England Mind* have emerged.[13] But an additional consequence has been that much of this later writing has lacked the comprehensiveness that gives *The New England Mind* its stature. There are signs of increasing dissatisfaction with the present fragmented approach, but no synthesis equal to Miller's is likely to appear soon. For many years to come every serious student of American Puritanism will still have to begin by reading *The New England Mind.*

Like many others considering research on American Puritanism I turned to *The New England Mind: The Seventeenth Century*. Dissatisfied with the incompleteness of its published documentation, I resorted, as some others have, to the unpublished notes to the volume that Perry Miller deposited at the Houghton Library at Harvard. The curator there, Martha Shaw, passed the bound, worn manuscript across the desk and said, "Someone should publish these." I gave her idea little thought at the time, sharing as I did the fairly common misimpression that the notes were not entirely reliable and that Miller had lost bibliographic control of his sources. But the notes turned out to be very accurate and reliable as a guide to the sources with which I was concerned, and I was interested in so many of the sources he had cited that, in addition to the work I had planned, it required only a little more effort to check his citations against all of the sources available at Houghton and Widener Libraries. I discovered that the notes as a whole were accurate, and it seemed to me that, as Ms. Shaw said, they were an important scholarly resource and should be published. Because *The New England Mind* remains our most comprehensive and coherent overview of American Puritanism, others for whom a trip to Houghton Library would not be convenient might wish to use the notes as a guide to Miller's sources. Moreover, publication would lay to rest some of the ill-founded rumors about Miller's deficiencies as a scholar.

Miller's notes were indeed accurate. Arbitrarily limiting verification to sources available at Houghton and Widener but nevertheless checking citations in the holdings of a few other libraries when my own research interests required it, I was able to check more than three-fourths of Miller's notes. The arbitrary limitation seemed justified, since extending the project to other libraries in, say, New England would have only slightly increased the number of notes checked, while attempting to verify every citation would have required a large expenditure of time and money in order to follow Miller's trail through European as well as American libraries. The result is that of Miller's 1,680 previously unpublished notes, I have checked 1,284 (counting notes with multiple citations as unchecked if not all sources could be verified). Among these I found only 26 errors, which puts Miller's accuracy rate at 1,258 out of 1,284, or a respectable 98 percent. Furthermore, many of the 26 errors were clerical or typographical. Usually the erroneous citations were "off" by only a page or two, except when the mistake was a typographical error in which a numeral was dropped (a reference, for instance, to page 54 of Charles Chauncy's *Plain Doctrin* instead of page 154).[14] In the notes as published here I have corrected silently 24 of the errors, while the 2 remaining mistakes are called to the user's attention immediately following those citations. Except for the correction of a few obvious typos in source titles, authors' names, and punctuation, no other changes have been made. The notes that have been checked, with the two exceptions mentioned, are to my best knowledge and ability correct as now published. Miller's scholarly responsibility having been established by the verification of three-fourths of the notes, those that remain unverified may be used, I believe, with as much confidence as those in most other books.

This is not to say, however, that there are no problems with Miller's documentation. He cannot be excused for his negligence in not even compiling unpublished notes for *The New England Mind: From Colony to Province.* By 1953, when that book was published, the importance of his work was well understood, and any publisher would have acceded if he had demanded inclusion of notes. Busily famous while continuing to be enormously productive, he never found the time to list his sources for that volume.[15] The younger Miller had the dedication to have found the time, and his not doing so in this case probably reflects some of the casual arrogance that glares from the pages of his later works. Even in *The New England Mind: The Seventeenth Century* there are dozens of quotations for which no source is given. Equally unsatisfactory is Miller's published explanation, that the notes to *The Seventeenth Century* were not published because "were I to supply a footnote indicating the exact source of every direct quotation or the inspiration for many remarks which are not literal citation, . . . the documentation would run to as many pages as the text."[16] It is not common to annotate "inspiration," and the sources of "direct quotation" deposited in Houghton Library would have added perhaps another seventy-five pages to *The Seventeenth Century*'s five hundred pages of text. A more likely explanation than Miller's is that the publisher wished to cut expenses in the closing years of the depression when *The Seventeenth Century* was published.[17] Even if the greatness of the book had been immediately recognized by the publisher, no one in 1939 could have imagined that it would still be in print four decades later and that it would be the central stimulus to making American Puritanism one of the most carefully and bountifully studied fields in all of American history. It is the success of Miller's books that makes the scholarly apparatus to *The New England Mind: The Seventeenth Century* important to a later generation.

Providing Miller's intellectual heirs with an accurate guide to his sources has been my principal objective in editing the notes for publication, but I could not help forming a general impression, also, of the accuracy and scrupulousness with which he quoted the sources in his text. Publication of these notes may permit others to settle the question more definitely, but for now my impression is that he was almost always true to the meaning and context of his sources. The instances where he did err seem to have been not only quite exceptional but also related to his persistent attempt to present a tension between the Puritans' general intellectual heritage and their pietistical ideas. This tendency may partly explain, for instance, the important misquotation in which he attributed to William Ames the position that the will is subject to the understanding. Norman Fiering, who found Miller's error, is surely right in saying that it could have been inadvertent, and, as Fiering notes, Miller quoted correctly other passages from Ames on the same question. But Miller had plenty of motivation, unconscious or otherwise, to not recognize his mistake since it provided an example of unresolved conflict between pietistical ideas and the intellectual heritage in the writing of one of the Puritans' most important authorities. The Puritans' intellectual heritage, according to Miller, taught that the will was always subject to the understanding, but their pietistical doctrine of regeneration required that the will retain some independence: "otherwise, once the reason had been rightly informed, the will would have no choice but to obey, and men could be made virtuous by good education instead of requiring the grace of God."[18]

Publication of these notes ought also to confirm respect for the size of Miller's sample. It is true that, as George Selement has pointed out, Miller exploited only a small fraction of extant New England documents such as "town, colony, and church records, creeds, laws, unpublished diaries, letters, sermons and sermon books, poems, histories, scientific journals, Latin exercises, legal briefs, even medical prescriptions, and Harvard theses."[19] But theology was the main focus of Miller's work because he believed it had been a more important factor in New England's history than Latin exercises. The absence of legal briefs and medical prescriptions is also understandable to those familiar with his insistence elsewhere that historians ought not take "unto themselves the prerogative of chronicling the life of the mind without distinguishing between the mind and the market place."[20] Given Miller's position that intellectual history is about people who could think rigorously, it is not surprising that he limited himself to published sources, mostly by educated New Englanders, mainly ministers. Selement estimates that for the period from 1620 to 1730 about 1,506 such sources are available to the historian.[21] However, if one takes into account that Miller was writing principally about New England orthodoxy, and not about Baptists, Quakers, or Anglicans, the appropriate number of published sources would be considerably less than 1,506. His citations to 223 different colonial sources, then, certainly constitute a significant sample, and of course he probably read some, perhaps many, other sources that he did not quote and therefore did not cite.[22] All this is in addition to his research in numerous English and Continental sources, especially on Ramist logic. Miller's sample in fact is so enormous that researching and writing an analytical and coherent book out of his vast materials would have been half a lifetime's work for most other mortals.

Selement has also criticized the representativeness of Miller's sources. While users of these notes will be able to settle that question for themselves, the fairness of Selement's argument deserves analysis, for the mere existence of his article has been accepted by some historians as sufficient or convincing evidence of *The New England Mind*'s unreliability.[23] Several scholars who had not read the article nevertheless mentioned it to me in attempting to discourage publication of Miller's notes. Yet a careful reading shows that there are major errors of interpretation in Selement's article, which makes it surprising that it has been given so much credence. To prove that Miller's source material "seems blatantly inadequate"[24] as a representative sample of New England thought, Selement calculated that 56 percent of Miller's 223 colonial sources and 68 percent of his 996 citations of colonial sources came from six ministers—Willard, Hooker, Cotton, Shepard, and Increase and Cotton Mather.[25] Selement's percentages are inflated, however, by his refusal to include Miller's 110 citations to Harvard theses, which Selement, in a footnote, calculates would reduce the six ministers' share from 56 percent to 37 percent of Miller's colonial sources.[26] Selement justifies his failure to include the Harvard theses in his calculations by asserting that little from them was incorporated into the text. Actually, Miller probably used a higher proportion of this scanty material than of any other source.[27] Yet if he did not rely as heavily on these six clergymen as Selement suggests, Miller did use them more than others, and with good reason: they were among the ablest writers of their time. Miller's literary standards would have inclined him to quote these authors even when he possessed similar evidence from other sources. Moreover, these six were far more prolific and prestigious than most other clergy, producing a disproportionate share of New England's writings and surely exercising a disproportionate influence on orthodox opinion. A solid history of orthodox ideas in seventeenth-century New England would normally lean more heavily on these ministers than on others. In short, the question of the representativeness of Miller's sources cannot be settled by mere counting.

Selement's criticism raises a still more troubling problem: namely, Selement's own irresponsible use of *his* major source, *The New England Mind*. For Selement, Miller's famous statement in the second paragraph of the foreword to *The Seventeenth Century* that he had treated New England expression "as though it were the product of a single intelligence" is proof of "Miller's disregard for historical *development* and *setting*" (my italics).[28] Yet in the preceding paragraph Miller made it clear that *The Seventeenth Century* was a "map of the intellectual terrain" or *setting* against which, in his second volume, he promised to attempt "a more sequential tracing of modifications and changes"— i.e., *development*.[29] He made good on that pledge in *From Colony to Province.* Yet because he argued there that change occurred "inside" the larger system of ideas outlined in the earlier volume, Selement characterizes the argument of *From Colony to Province* as a "contention that Puritan thought remained basically static between 1630 and 1730." This is a misrepresentation of the major point of *From Colony to Province,* which is that gradual, apparently harmless change "inside" established ideas had metamorphosed those ideas, especially covenant theory, by 1730. Nevertheless, as final proof that Miller omitted "evolutionary progression," Selement switches back, without saying so in his text, to *The Seventeenth Century* and quotes Miller himself: "The topical method of *this volume* . . . has most notably obscured the chronology of the situation" (my italics).[30] Thus, a reader may easily think that by "this volume" Miller is referring to *From Colony to Province,* where he had promised a chronological treatment but seems now to be admitting to failure. There is little point in multiplying such examples from Selement's article, but it could be done easily.[31]

Selement "seems" (one of his favorite words) to realize that there are some large holes in his argument, and he occasionally attempts to give Miller the benefit of the doubt. Surely, he reasons, a historian of Miller's accomplishments knew of Separatists, Baptists, and Quakers and could not have meant that all New Englanders were in "absolute agreement." "Instead, he seems to have meant that an 'orthodoxy' prevailed in New England, encompassing a majority of the ministers." (The effort involved in these deductions might have been saved by citing Miller's statement that "few Puritans ever agreed on every feature of it [their philosophy], and on some essentials there was always difficulty in framing a formula satisfactory to all the orthodox.") If Miller was writing about the orthodox, says Selement, then it was "logical" for him to have used "limited source materials." But if Miller's use of his sources was satisfactory after all, then what is the point of Selement's article analyzing those sources? Selement's solution to this problem is to state that Miller's "error" lay not in his use of sources but "in his failure to inform readers" that he was dealing with "a select group [that is, the orthodox majority] of ministers."[32] Surely most readers have been happier for not having been "informed" of something so obvious on every page of *The New England Mind.*

Notes

1. George Bancroft, *A History of the United States,* 10 vols. (Boston, 1834-1875); John Gorham Palfrey, *History of New England,* 5 vols. (Boston, 1858-1890); Brooks Adams, *The Emancipation of Massachusetts* (Boston, 1887); George Santayana, *The Genteel Tradition: Nine Essays,* ed. Douglas L. Wilson (Cambridge, Mass., 1967); Van Wyck Brooks, *The Wine of the Puritans: A Study of Present-Day America* (London, 1908); H. L. Mencken, "Puritanism as a Literary Force," in Mencken, *A Book of Prefaces* (New York, 1917), 197-283; James Truslow Adams, *The Founding of New England* (Boston, 1921).

2. Perry Miller, *Orthodoxy in Massachusetts, 1630-1650: A Genetic Study* (Cambridge, Mass., 1933), xi. This book has stirred a controversy as to the degree to which the Bay settlers had elaborated their system of ecclesiastical polity before leaving England. But Miller's largest idea—that they were Congregationalists in principle and that their motives for coming to New England included a desire to implement that principle—remains unchallenged. See Edmund S. Morgan, *Visible Saints: The History of a Puritan Idea* (New York, 1963), 81*ff.,* and David D. Hall's introduction to the 1970 reprint of Miller, *Orthodoxy in Massachusetts* (New York, 1970), xvii.

3. Samuel Eliot Morison, *Builders of the Bay Colony* (Boston, 1930); Kenneth Ballard Murdock, *Increase Mather: The Foremost American Puritan* (Cambridge, Mass., 1925).

4. Samuel Eliot Morison, *The Founding of Harvard College* (Cambridge, Mass., 1935); Morison, *Harvard College in the Seventeenth Century,* 2 vols. (Cambridge, Mass., 1936).

5. Perry Miller, *The New England Mind: The Seventeenth Century* (New York, 1939), 440.

6. *Ibid.,* 9, 108. For a more detailed discussion of this tension, see James Hoopes, "Art as History: Perry Miller's *New England Mind,*" *American Quarterly,* forthcoming.

7. Miller, *The New England Mind: The Seventeenth Century,* 396. Everett H. Emerson has convincingly argued that Miller overestimated the degree to which Puritan covenant theory was a compromise with original, and supposedly sterner, Calvinism. This suggests that Miller may also have overestimated the absoluteness of the Puritans' pietistical ideas, for his description of those ideas was meant to place Puritans in what he thought of as the Calvinist tradition. Emerson's article thus weakens the supposed tension between pietistical ideas and the intellectual heritage that is Miller's primary theme. But even so, it was a great achievement to recover the Puritans' intellectual heritage. Until a superior but equally comprehensive account of that heritage appears, Miller's book will continue to be the basic text on American Puritan ideas. Emerson, "Calvin and the Covenant Theology," *Church History,* XXV (1956), 136-144.

8. Miller, *The New England Mind: The Seventeenth Century,* 396, 399-400.

9. *Ibid.*, 397, 400.

10. Edmund S. Morgan, "Perry Miller and the Historians," American Antiquarian Society, *Proceedings,* LXXIV (1964), 18.

11. David Hollinger, "Perry Miller and Philosophical History,"*History and Theory,* VII (1968), 200.

12. David D. Hall, "Understanding the Puritans," in Herbert J. Bass, ed., *The State of American History* (Chicago, 1970), 349.

13. Among the best recent studies in New England Puritanism are Sacvan Bercovitch, "Typology in Puritan New England: The Williams-Cotton Controversy Reassessed," *Am. Qtly.*, XIX (1967), 166-191; Norman Fiering, *Moral Philosophy at Seventeenth-Century Harvard: A Discipline in Transition* (Chapel Hill, N.C., 1981); David D. Hall, *The Faithful Shepherd: A History of the New England Ministry in the Seventeenth Century* (Chapel Hill, N.C., 1972); E. Brooks Holifield, *The Covenant Sealed: The Development of Puritan Sacramental Theology in Old and New England, 1570-1720* (New Haven, Conn., 1974); and William K. B. Stoever, *"A Faire and Easie Way to Heaven": Covenant Theology and Antinomianism in Early Massachusetts* (Middletown, Conn., 1978). All of these works correct, extend, or offer alternative theses to Miller's. None of them, however, are comprehensive enough to offer an alternative synthesis to that of *The New England Mind.*

14. Miller, *The New England Mind: The Seventeenth Century,* 65.

15. Interview with Elizabeth Miller, June 1979.

16. Miller, *The New England Mind: The Seventeenth Century,* "Foreword."

17. Interview with Elizabeth Miller, June 1979.

18. Norman S. Fiering, "Will and Intellect in the New England Mind," *William and Mary Quarterly,* 3d Ser., XXIX (1972), 532-533; Miller, *The New England Mind: The Seventeenth Century,* 248-249. Fiering repeats this discussion in *Moral Philosophy at Harvard,* chap. 3.

Miller's misquotation of Cotton Mather, discovered by Robert Middlekauff, could have a similar explanation. Miller may have inadvertently written "Conversion" rather than "Conversation" in taking his notes. But by having Mather speak of entering the covenant as an influence toward "Conversion," Miller seemed to clinch his statements as to Mather's Arminianism, which Miller believed resulted from the "expanding limits of natural ability" as the intellectual heritage triumphed over pietistical ideas. Miller, *The New England Mind: From Colony to Province* (Cambridge, Mass., 1953), 67; Robert Middlekauff, *The Mathers: Three Generations of Puritan Intellectuals, 1596-1728* (New York, 1971), 241.

19. George Selement, "Perry Miller: A Note on His Sources in *The New England Mind: The Seventeenth Century,*" WMQ, 3d Ser., XXXI (1974), 455.

20. Perry Miller, ed., *American Thought: Civil War to World War I* (New York, 1954), vii.

21. Selement, "Perry Miller," WMQ, 3d Ser., XXXI (1974), 455.

22. Perry Miller and Thomas H. Johnson, eds., *The Puritans: A Sourcebook of Their Writings* (New York, 1938) demonstrates an amazing grasp of the full breadth of Puritan writing.

23. See, for example, James A. Henretta, "Social History as Lived and Written," *American Historical Review,* LXXXIV (1979), 1317n.

24. Selement, "Perry Miller," WMQ, 3d Ser., XXXI (1974), 456. Selement refers here only to Miller's sources for the latter part of the 17th century. But Selement takes a similar view of Miller's research for the earlier part of the century and says it failed "to fulfill rigorous standards for a definitive study" (p. 455). Selement does not specify the standards needed for a definitive study.

25. *Ibid.,* 456-457.

26. *Ibid.,* 457n.

27. Even if Selement's assertion were correct it would indicate little more than that the only way Miller could have avoided Selement's criticism for not exploiting medical prescriptions would have been by quoting from them at the same length in his text as he did, say, from Willard's *Compleat Body of Divinity.*

28. Selement, "Perry Miller," WMQ, 3d Ser., XXXI (1974), 458.

29. Miller, *The New England Mind: The Seventeenth Century,* "Foreword."

30. Selement, "Perry Miller," WMQ, 3d Ser., XXXI (1974), 463. Selement does indicate his switch of sources in a footnote.

31. See Selement's two paragraphs on Miller's treatment of Puritan logic (*ibid.*, 457-458), which contain several instances of faulty argument. For example, Selement quotes Morison that the Harvard theses "must be used with caution" and then concludes that since Miller used the theses "his reliability is questionable." Of course the real issue, which Selement avoids, is whether or not Miller used the theses appropriately and with the care Morison advised. It should be noted also that this criticism of Miller for using the theses contradicts Selement's earlier emphasis (p. 455) on the need to use the broadest possible range of sources, including, he specifically says, the Harvard theses!

32. *Ibid.*, 458; Miller, *The New England Mind: The Seventeenth Century*, 90-91.

Bibliographical Note

ADDITIONAL information on Miller and his work may be found in the following:

Crowell, John C. "Perry Miller as Historian: A Bibliography of Evaluations." *Bulletin of Bibliography and Magazine Notes,* XXXIV (1977), 77-85. An annotated list of publications by and about Miller.

Hall, David D. "Understanding the Puritans." In Herbert J. Bass, ed., *The State of American History.* Chicago, 1970. An analysis of weaknesses in *The New England Mind* with suggestions for future scholarship.

Hollinger, David. "Perry Miller and Philosophical History." *History and Theory,* VII (1968), 189-202. A searching analysis of the personal philosophy revealed in Miller's writings.

Hoopes, James. "Art as History: Perry Miller's *New England Mind.*" *American Quarterly,* forthcoming. A close reading of *The New England Mind* and some of its critics.

Miller, Perry. *The Responsibility of Mind in a Civilization of Machines: Essays by Perry Miller,* ed. John Crowell and Stanford J. Searl, Jr. Amherst, Mass., 1980. Contains some biographical information on Miller.

Morgan, Edmund S. "The Historians of Early New England." In Ray Allen Billington, ed., *The Reinterpretation of Early American History: Essays in Honor of John Edwin Pomfret.* San Marino, Calif., 1966. Places Miller's work in the context of early New England historiography.

Wise, Gene. *American Historical Explanations: A Strategy for Grounded Inquiry.* Homewood, Ill., 1973. Treats *The New England Mind: From Colony to Province* as a model for relating ideas to society.

Key to the Sources

MILLER prepared a typescript of his notes and then superscribed reference numerals at appropriate points in a printed copy of *The New England Mind: The Seventeenth Century*, which he filed in Houghton Library with the notes. Until now the notes have been useless without that special copy of the book. In order to make the notes generally usable, they are here keyed to the text by page and line. Because all three editions (Macmillan, 1939; Harvard, 1954; Beacon Paperback, 1961) have the same pagination, this system permits the notes to be used with any of them.

An arrow indicates whether one should count down from the top of the page or up from the bottom, while the number following the arrow indicates the line to which the note refers. An asterisk following the line number indicates that a note could not be checked against holdings in Houghton or Widener Libraries. In the case of notes containing more than one citation, the asterisk, if it appears alone, indicates that none of the citations in the note could be checked. When all but one citation in a note could be checked, the unchecked citation is indicated immediately after the asterisk by a number in parentheses that refers to the sequence of the citation in the note. The arrow, the number, and, in some cases, the asterisk or the citation number are followed by the word or words that immediately precede Miller's reference numerals in his marked copy, as in the following examples from page 130 of Miller's text:

↓ 2   truth   Stone, <u>A Congregational Church is a Catholike Visible Church</u>, p. F3 recto.

The citation of Stone refers to the second line down, at the end of the quotation concluding with the word "truth."

↓18* so   Anthony Wotton, <u>The Art of Logick</u> (London, 1626), p. 108.

The citation of Wotton, marked by an asterisk, could not be checked.

↑ 6*(2)Reasoning James Fitch, <u>First Principles</u>, pp. 57-59; <u>An Explanation of the Solemn Advice</u> (1683), p. 81.

Of the two Fitch sources referred to after "Reasoning" in the sixth line from the bottom of the page, the *First Principles* was checked but the *Explanation* could not be.

Comparative (cf.) references were checked when they constituted the entire note but not when they were offered in support of another source.

A few works owned by Houghton or Widener were not checked because they were off the shelf at the time requested. Some references to readily available works by Aristotle, Augustine, and other authors of similar rank were not checked because Miller did not indicate the editions he used.

A number of apparent inconsistencies, where one citation was checked but another to the same source was not, are due to imperfect editions in the possession of Houghton or Widener Libraries.

Sources for THE NEW ENGLAND MIND:
THE SEVENTEENTH CENTURY

Unless otherwise indicated, works of New England authors were printed at Boston.

Citations of Harvard theses from the commencement of 1642 refer to Appendix D of Samuel Eliot Morison, *The Founding of Harvard College* (Cambridge, Mass., 1935). Theses and Quaestiones from later commencements through 1708 are taken from Appendix B of Morison, *Harvard College in the Seventeenth Century* (Cambridge, Mass., 1936).

Chapter I: The Augustinian Strain of Piety

p.   3

↓11* eye   Augustine, Confessions, III, 10.

p.   4

↓ 4 made   Thomas Hooker, The Application of Redemption (London,
                    1659), pp. 380-381.

p.   7

↓13 evidenceth   Hooker, Application of Redemption, p. 694.

↓14 men   Hooker, A Survey of the Summe of Church-Discipline
                    (London, 1648), pt. I, p. 79.

↑19 whirlwind   John Allin, "The Lord Jesus, His Legacy of Peace"
                    (Cambridge, 1672), in E. Burgess, The Dedham Pulpit
                    (Boston, 1840), p. 23.

↑11* God   Increase Mather, A Discourse Concerning Earthquakes
                    (1706), p. 43.

p.   8

↓ 7 control   Samuel Willard, Mercy Magnified on a penitent Prodigal
                    (1684), p. 145.

↑ 6* omnino   Augustine, Soliloquies, I, 7.

p.   9

↑ 3 creature   John Davenport, Preface to Henry Scudder, The Christians
                    Daily Walke (London, 1635), p. A3 recto.

p.   10

↑ 4 Being   John Preston, Life Eternall (London, 1634), pt. I, p. 94.

↑ 1 immediately   Preston, The New Covenant (London, 1629), p. 503.

p.   11

↓ 1 earth   Ibid., p. 111.

p.   11 continued

↓ 5   hand   Preston, Life Eternall, pt. I, p. 102.

↓11   behold it   Thomas Shepard, Works (ed. John A. Albro, Boston, 1853),
                           I, 14.

↓17   Object   Willard, A Compleat Body of Divinity (1726), p. 42.

↓21   himselfe   William Ames, The Marrow of Sacred Divinity (London,
                           1643), p. 11.

↑13   nature   Ibid.

↑ 9   it   Willard, Compleat Body, p. 50.

↑ 5   objects   Shepard, Works, I, 14, 15.

p.   12

↓ 1* conceiving   John Norton, A Brief and Excellent Treatise Containing
                           the Doctrine of Godlines (London, 1648), p. 10; cf. The
                           Orthodox Evangelist (London, 1654), p. 3.

↓ 4* God   Norton, A Brief and Excellent Treatise, p. 10.

↓18   omnipotency   Norton, Orthodox Evangelist, pp. 4-20.

↑ 8   wisedome   Preston, Life Eternall, pt. II, p. 53; cf. pt. II, p. 180

↑ 3   contrarily   Willard, Compleat Body, p. 51.

p.   13

↓10   another   James Fitch, The first Principles of the Doctrine of
                           Christ (1679), p. 7.

p.   14

↓ 5   not be   Hooker, Application of Redemption, pp. 380, 394.

↑11   all   Increase Mather, The Doctrine of Divine Providence
                           (1684), p. 21.

↑ 6   it   Urian Oakes, The Soveraign Efficacy of Divine Providence
                           (1682), p. 17.

p.　14 continued

↑ 2　them　　　　　Willard, Compleat Body, p. 105; cf. p. 107.

p.　15

↓ 3　creation　　　Adolph Harnack, History of Dogma (Boston, 1899-1902),
　　　　　　　　　　V, 121, 122; cf. John Cotton, A Practical Commentary. . .
　　　　　　　　　　upon The First Epistle Generall of John (London, 1656),
　　　　　　　　　　p. 267.

↓ 9* end　　　　　Hooker, An Exposition of the Principles of Religion
　　　　　　　　　　(London, 1645), p. 5.

↓21　work　　　　　William Adams, God's Eye on the Contrite (1685), pp. 6-7.

↓24　therein　　　Increase Mather, Doctrine of Divine Providence, p. 11.

↑18　Intention　　Willard, Compleat Body, p. 104.

↑11　consequences　Willard, The Checkered State of the Gospel Church
　　　　　　　　　　(1701), p. 40.

↑ 3　Earth　　　　Increase Mather, A Discourse Concerning the Uncertainty
　　　　　　　　　　of the Times of Men (1697), pp. 17-18.

p.　16

↓ 4* matters　　　Increase Mather, Some Important Truths Concerning
　　　　　　　　　　Conversion (2 ed., 1684), p. 91.

↓ 5　frivolity　　Increase Mather, A Testimony Against several Prophane
　　　　　　　　　　and Superstitious Customs (London, 1687), pp. 12-13;
　　　　　　　　　　cf. Ames, Marrow, bk. II, ch. 11.

↑19　Hand　　　　　Oakes, Soveraign Efficacy, p. 12.

↑12　logic　　　　Willard, Compleat Body, p. 103.

↑10　choice　　　　Ames, Marrow, p. 32.

↑ 8* will　　　　　Norton, A Brief and Excellent Treatise, p. 22.

p.　17

↓19　displayed　　Willard, The Truly Blessed Man (1700), p. 311.

p.   17 continued

↓23 glory   Preston, <u>Life Eternall</u>, pt. I, p. 145.

↑12 left   Willard, <u>Useful Instructions for a professing People</u> (Cambridge, 1673), p. 26.

p.   18

↓ 6 them   Willard, <u>Compleat Body</u>, p. 76.

↓12* iust   William Perkins, <u>Works</u>, I (London, 1626), p. 278.

↑17 exception   Preston, <u>Life Eternall</u>, pt. I, pp. 143-144.

↑14 things   Shepard, <u>Works</u>, I, 340; John Davenport and William Hook <u>A Catechisme</u> (London, 1659), pp. 9-10.

↑12 do it   Willard, <u>Mercy Magnified</u>, p. 253.

p.   19

↓ 3* Thee   Augustine, <u>Confessions</u>, VII, 18; cf. <u>City of God</u>, XI, 18, 23.

↓ 9 him   Preston, <u>New Covenant</u>, p. 162.

↓15 will   Norton, <u>The Heart of N-England rent at the Blasphemies of the Present Generation</u> (Cambridge, 1659), p. 29.

↓17 manifest   Norton, <u>Orthodox Evangelist</u>, p. 120.

↑22 come   Cotton, <u>A Briefe Exposition with Practicall Observation upon The Whole Book of Ecclesiastes</u> (London, 1654), pp. 191-193.

↑13 disquietnesse <u>Ibid</u>.

↑ 6* exemption   Thomas Cobbett, <u>A Fruitfull and Usefull Discourse</u> (London, 1656), p. 13.

p.   20

↓ 9 upon   Ames, <u>Marrow</u>, p. 9; cf. p. 72.

↓17 confirmations Cf. Willard, <u>Compleat Body</u>, pp. 17-20.

p.   20 continued

↓20* Scripture   Davenport, <u>The Knowledge of Christ Indispensably</u>
                  <u>required of all men that would be saved</u> (London, 1653),
                  p. 80.

↑21 <u>Demonstration</u> Cotton Mather, <u>Christianus per Ignem</u> (1702), p. 46.

↑18 thee   Hooker, "The Poore Doubting Christian," in <u>The Saints</u>
                  <u>Cordials</u> (London, 1629), p. 355.

↑15 that   Shepard, <u>Works</u>, I, 140.

↑13* God   Davenport, <u>The Saints Anchor-Hold</u> (London, 1661), p. 133.

↑11 himself   Samuel Lee, <u>The Joy of Faith</u> (1687), p. 59.

p.   21

↓10* word   Hooker, <u>Heavens Treasury Opened</u> (London, 1645), pp. 67-68.

↓14 things   Willard, <u>Walking with God</u> (1701), p. 28.

↓17 contradictory Willard, <u>Compleat Body</u>, p. 325.

↓19 actions   Cotton, <u>Christ the Fountaine of Life</u> (London, 1651),
                  p. 211.

↓22 blindness   Increase Mather, <u>The Mystery of Christ</u> (1686), p. 44.

↓23 Scriptures   Cotton, <u>Of the Holinesse of Church-Members</u> (London,
                  1650), p. 77; cf. Ames, <u>Marrow</u>, p. 191.

p.   22

↓20* it   Augustine, <u>Confessions</u>, VII, 20.

↓24* unlawful   <u>Ibid</u>., II, 14; cf. VII, 21, 22; cf. also Harnack,
                  <u>History of Dogma</u>, V, 66-76.

↑ 8* <u>will</u> Hooker, "Preparing for Christ," p. 68, in <u>The Unbeleevers</u>
                  <u>Preparing for Christ</u> (London, 1638); cf. Increase Mather,
                  <u>Solemn Advice to Young Men</u> (1695), p. 12.

p.   23

↓ 5   center   Davenport, Preface to Scudder, The Christians Daily
                    Walke, p. A5 verso.

↓10   man   Hooker, The Soules Humiliation (London, 1638), p. 34.

↓21   dwells   Anne Bradstreet, Works (ed. John Harvard Ellis,
                    Charlestown, 1867), p. 61.

↓23   carkasse   Davenport, Preface to Scudder, The Christians Daily
                    Walke, p. A6 verso.

↑ 3   expected   Hooker, Application of Redemption, pp. 610-611.

p.   24

↓ 1   them   Cotton, A Practical Commentary . . . upon The First
                    Epistle Generall of John, p. 112.

↓ 9   sight   Hooker, Application of Redemption, pp. 46, 52.

↓12   himself   Hooker, Soules Humiliation, p. 121.

↓17   relief   Hooker, Application of Redemption, p. 412.

↑13   maker   Willard, Compleat Body, p. 246.

↑ 5   Apostacy   Ibid., p. 158; cf. pp. 224ff.

p.   25

↓14   in   Ibid., p. 157.

↑14   Spirit   John Ball, A Treatise of Faith (London, 1632), pp. 11-1

p.   26

↓ 4   man   Hooker, Preface to John Rogers, The Doctrine of Faith
                    (London, 1629), p. A8 recto.

↓13   great   Hooker, The Soules Exaltation (London, 1638), p. 25.

p.   27

↓ 7   committed   Ibid., p. 117; cf. Willard, Compleat Body, pp. 462ff.

p.　27 continued

↓14　writers　　　　William Chappell, <u>The Preacher, or the Art and Method of Preaching</u> (London, 1656), Appendix.

↑16　heart　　　　　Hooker, <u>Soules Exaltation</u>, pp. 140-141.

↑12　thereof　　　　Hooker, <u>A Comment upon Christ's last Prayer</u> (London, 1656), p. 88.

↑ 2　nature　　　　　Cotton, <u>The New Covenant</u> (London, 1654), p. 182.

p.　28

↓ 1　from another　Hooker, <u>The Soules Implantation</u> (London, 1637), p. 10.

↓ 4　part　　　　　<u>Ibid</u>., p. 86.

↓ 8　God　　　　　　Hooker, <u>The Soules Vocation</u> (London, 1638), pp. 396-397.

↓10　sin　　　　　　Fitch, <u>First Principles</u>, pp. 44-45.

↑14　us　　　　　　　Ball, <u>Treatise of Faith</u>, p. 9.

↑12* hearts　　　　Davenport, <u>Saints Anchor-Hold</u>, pp. 100-101.

↑ 7　obedience　　William Hubbard, <u>The Benefit of a Well-Ordered Conversation</u> (1684), pp. 12-13.

p.　29

↓ 7　thereof　　　　Shepard, <u>Works</u>, II, 286-287.

↓11　advantage　　Preston, <u>The Saints Qualification</u> (London, 1633), pp. 152-153; Ames, <u>Marrow</u>, p. 129.

↓19　contend　　　　Preston, <u>Saints Qualification</u>, p. 161.

↑14　businesse　　Cotton, <u>Christ the Fountaine of Life</u>, p. 110.

p.　30

↓ 7　<u>not to be</u>　Norton, <u>Heart of N-England rent</u>, p. 12.

↓13* light　　　　Preston, <u>The Deformed Forme of a Formall Profession</u> (Edinburgh, 1632), p. A4 recto.

p.   30 continued

↑15 are   Shepard, Works, I, 127.

↑14 dead life   Cotton, The way of Life (London, 1641), p. 301.

↑10 dead   Ibid. pp. 217, 222.

↑ 7 nature   Charles Chauncy, The Plain Doctrin of the Justificatic
                                of a Sinner in the sight of God (London, 1659), p. 145

↑ 1 secured   Preston, Saints Qualification, pp. 127-128.

p.   31

↓11 himselfe   Rogers, Doctrine of Faith, p. 6.

↓17 spirit   Hooker, The Saints Dignitie, and Dutie (London, 1651),
                                pp. 208-209.

↑12 now   Ibid., pp. 210-211.

↑10 heaven   Ibid., pp. 207-208.

p.   32

↓ 5 them   Hooker, The Saints Guide (London, 1645), pp. 33-34.

↓ 9 faith   Hooker, Application of Redemption, pp. 98-99.

↓12 alone   Cotton, An Exposition upon The Thirteenth Chapter of
                                the Revelation (London, 1656), pp. 118-119.

↓19 Institution   Samuel Mather, A Testimony from the Scripture against
                                Idolatry & Superstition (Cambridge, 1670), p. 16.

↑19 darkness   Norton, Heart of N-England rent, p. 13.

↑12 darkness   Ibid.,; cf. Shepard, Works, II, 282-283.

p.   33

↑22 himself   Hooker, Application of Redemption, pp. 3-4.

↑20 move   Shepard, Works, I, 168.

p.   33 continued

↑15   Work   Hooker, <u>Application of Redemption</u>, p. 4.

↑ 10 Called   John Rogers, <u>A Sermon Preached before His Excellency the</u>
                         <u>Governour. . .</u> (1706), p. 9.

p.   34

↓ 9   hypocrite   Shepard, <u>Works</u>, II, 212-213; cf. II, 52-53.

Chapter II: The Practice of Piety

<u>p.   36</u>

↓19   talk   Thomas Hooker, <u>The Application of Redemption</u> (London, 1659), p. 154.

↓22   affliction   John Cotton, <u>The way of Life</u> (London, 1641), p. 477.

↑10   Confusion   Samuel Willard, <u>A Compleat Body of Divinity</u> (1726), p. 121.

↑ 7   Death   Jonathan Mitchell, <u>A Discourse of the Glory To which God hath called Believers by Jesus Christ</u> (London, 1677), p. 66.

↑ 5   Dunghil   Cotton, <u>A Practical Commentary . . . upon The First Epistle Generall of John</u> (London, 1656), p. 120.

↑ 4* them   Increase Mather, <u>Two Plain and Practical Discourses Concerning Hardness of Heart</u> (London, 1699), p. 18.

<u>p.   37</u>

↑22   other   Cotton, <u>Way of Life</u>, p. 205.

↑18   sea   Joshua Moody, <u>Souldiery Spiritualized</u> (Cambridge, 1674), p. 20.

↑13   other   Urian Oakes, <u>The Unconquerable, All-Conquering, & more-then-Conquering Souldier</u> (Cambridge, 1674), p. 12

<u>p.   38</u>

↑18   extasies   Willard, <u>The Child's Portion</u> (1684), <u>passim</u>.

↑13   sake   Cotton, <u>A Discourse about Civil Government in a New Plantation Whose Design is Religion</u>. (Cambridge, 1663; attributed to John Davenport), p. 15.

↑11* Elect   John Norton, <u>A Brief and Excellent Treatise Containing the Doctrine of Godlines</u> (London, 1648), p. 25.

<u>p.   39</u>

↓ 1   affliction   Cf. Willard, <u>Compleat Body</u>, p. 746 ff.

↓10   Endeavours   Oakes, <u>The Soveraign Efficacy of Divine Providence</u> (1682), p. 10.

p.   39 continued

↓12 here   Increase Mather, The Doctrine of Divine Providence
                     (1684), p. 43.

↓18 it   Cotton, An Exposition upon The Thirteenth Chapter of
                     the Revelation (London, 1656), p. 78.

↓21* God   Increase Mather, The Times of men are in the hand of
                     God (1675), p. 7.

↑19 Afflictions   Benjamin Wadsworth, Considerations To Prevent Murmuring
                     and Promote Patience in Christians, Under Afflictive
                     Providences (1706), p. 6.

↑18* world   Willard, The Just Man's Prerogative (1706), p. 10.

↑15 Vexations   Cotton Mather, Seven Select Lectures (London, 1695),
                     p. 124.

↑10* therein   John Davenport, The Saints Anchor-Hold (London, 1661),
                     p. 121.

p.   40

↓ 5* confusion   Zacharias Ursinus, The Summe of Christian Religion
                     (tr. Henry Passy, London, 1633), p. 208.

↓22 Spirit   Joshua Moody, A Practical Discourse Concerning the
                     Choice Benefit of Communion with God in His House
                     (1746), p. 13.

p.   41

↓11 being   Cotton, Way of Life, p. 436.

↓16* made   Willard, Just Man's Prerogative, p. 6.

↓17 Sabbath   E.g. Cotton Mather, Christianus per Ignem (1702),
                     p. 110.

↓21* it   Willard, Just Man's Prerogative, p. 8.

↑18* more   John Danforth, The Right Christian Temper (1702),
                     p. 3.

p. 41 continued

↑ 8 licentiousness Willard, <u>The Christians Exercise by Satans Temptations</u>
(1701), p. 121.

p. 42

↓18 spirit John Preston, <u>Life Eternall</u> (London, 1634), pt. II,
p. 6.

↓20 Devil Increase Mather, <u>Wo to Drunkards</u> (Cambridge, 1673),
p. 4.

↑13 <u>not</u> Preston, <u>Life Eternall</u>, pt. II, p. 57.

↑ 6 in you Cotton, <u>A Practical Commentary . . . upon The First
Epistle Generall of John</u>, p. 110.

p. 43

↓ 6 it Cotton, <u>Christ the Fountaine of Life</u> (London, 1651),
p. 119.

p. 44

↓ 7 labourer Cotton, <u>Way of Life</u>, pp. 437-438.

↓11 beast <u>Ibid</u>., p. 449.

↓14 Work-house John Bailey, <u>Man's chief End To Glorifie God</u> (1689),
p. 64.

↓16 mind Cotton, <u>Way of Life</u>, pp. 443, 451; cf. also discussion
of "calling" in John Ball, <u>A Treatise of Faith</u> (London
1632), pp. 387-399.

↑15 employments Thomas Shepard, <u>Works</u> (ed. John A. Albro, Boston,
1853), I, 306.

p. 45

↑ 4* <u>Evil</u> Cotton Mather, <u>The Armour of Christianity</u> (1704),
p. 51.

.	46	
6	naught	Hooker, The Christians Two Chiefe Lessons (London, 1640), p. 216.
8	also	Richard Mather, Church-Government and Church-Covenant Discussed (London, 1643), Preface.
10	Immortality	Cotton, Christ the Fountaine of Life, p. 47.
13*	Name	Hooker, Heavens Treasury Opened (London, 1645), p. 39.
16	himself	Cotton, A Practical Commentary . . . upon The First Epistle Generall of John, p. 233.
21	head	Samuel Mather, A Testimony from the Scripture against Idolatry & Superstition (Cambridge, 1670), p. 17.
17	consider	Ibid., p. 67.
.	47	
3	spirited	Mitchell, Discourse of the Glory, pp. 225-226.
16	grace	Hooker, The Soules Humiliation (London, 1638), p. 77.
.	48	
14	use	William Ames, The Marrow of Sacred Divinity (London, 1643), p. 157; cf. pp. 2-3.
15	part	Preston, The New Covenant (London, 1629), p. 61; cf. The Breast-Plate of Faith and Love (London, 1634), pt. III, p. 200.
18	intend	Hooker, Application of Redemption, p. 183.
20	Performances	Willard, Compleat Body, p. 456.
13	worke	Preston, A Sermon Preached at a Generall Fast before the Commons-House of Parliament (London, 1633), p. 292.
11	teacher	Hooker, The Soules Exaltation (London, 1638), p. 110.

p.　48 continued

↑ 8　planting　　　Hooker, The Soules Implantation (London, 1637), p. 158

p.　49

↓ 4* sanctified　　Hooker, Heavens Treasury Opened, p. 122; cf. Ames, Marrow, pp. ·125 ff.

↓ 9　secret　　　　Hooker, The Saints Dignitie, and Dutie (London, 1651), p. 166.

↑ 4　accomplished　Preston, Sinnes Overthrow (London, 1635), pp. 14-15.

p.　50

↓ 7　doctrine　　　John Rogers, The Doctrine of Faith (London, 1629), pp. 35-36.

↓17　of it　　　　Cotton, Way of Life, p. 319.

↓20　grace　　　　Cotton, Christ the Fountaine of Life, p. 190.

↑ 4　him　　　　　Willard, Child's Portion, p. 90.

p.　51

↓ 7　it　　　　　Rogers, Doctrine of Faith, pp. 355-357.

↓11　tests　　　　Ames, Marrow, pp. 131-132.

↓14　grace　　　　Hooker, Saints Dignitie, p. 74.

↓20　sweet　　　　Shepard, Works, II, 222.

↑19　Child　　　　Cotton, A Practical Commentary . . . upon The First Epistle Generall of John, p. 196.

↑15　reformation　Hooker, Soules Humiliation, p. 154.

↑ 9　justified　　Cotton, A Practical Commentary . . . upon The First Epistle Generall of John, p. 62.

↑ 5　evident　　　Cotton, The New Covenant (London, 1654), pp. 76-77.

p.   52

↓14   differ   Cotton, <u>A Treatise of the Covenant of Grace</u> (London, 1671), p. 39.

↓16   Justification   Cotton, <u>New Covenant</u>, p. 64.

↓21   sanctification Shepard, <u>Works</u>, I, 95-99; II, 282-287; II, 472 ff.

↑19   them   Cotton, <u>New Covenant</u>, pp. 64-65.

↑16* God   Davenport, <u>Saints Anchor-Hold</u>, pp. 109 ff.

↑ 9   outrages   Preston, <u>The Saints Qualification</u> (London, 1633), pp. 126-127.

↑ 5   owne   Hooker, <u>The Christians Two Chiefe Lessons</u>, p. 213.

↑ 2   young   Shepard, <u>Works</u>, I, 65.

p.   53

↓ 3   afterwards   Hooker, "The Poore Doubting Christian," in <u>The Saints Cordials</u> (London, 1629), p. 365.

↓18   heart   Peter Bulkeley, <u>The Gospel-Covenant</u> (London, 1651), p. 340.

↓20   soule   Hooker, <u>The Soules Preparation for Christ</u> (London, 1638), p. 79.

↑17   God   Mitchell, <u>Discourse of the Glory</u>, p. 210.

p.   54

↓18   degrees   Ames, <u>Marrow</u>, p. 115.

↑14   out   John Ball, <u>A Treatise of Faith</u>, p. 92.

↑ 3   hearts   Hooker, <u>The Christians Two Chiefe Lessons</u>, pp. 210-211.

p.   55

↓ 2   again   Mitchell, <u>Discourse of the Glory</u>, p. 72.

p.   55 continued

↓ 6 Ebb   Ibid., p. 73.

↑20 Christ   Hooker, The Soules Vocation (London, 1638), p. 186.

↑ 4 prayers   Hooker, Soules Humiliation, p. 41.

↑ 2 here   Ibid., p. 116; cf. pp. 186-190.

p.   56

↓ 6 him   Hooker, Application of Redemption, pp. 666-667.

↓15 it   Ibid., p. 214.

↓19 it   Ibid., p. c3 recto.

↑ 6 conscience   Cotton, A Practical Commentary . . . upon The First
                        Epistle Generall of John, p. 1.

p.   57

↑ 5 him   Hooker, Soules Humiliation, p. 117.

↑ 1* glory   Hooker, Heavens Treasury Opened, p. 41.

p.   58

↓10 vessell   Hooker, Soules Preparation, p. 107.

↑ 1 fooles   Hooker, Soules Implantation, pp. 215-218.

p.   59

↓10 sweat   Hooker, The Christians Two Chiefe Lessons, p. 64.

↓14 for   Cotton, Way of Life, pp. 120-121.

↓20 point   Moody, Souldiery Spiritualized, p. 7.

p.   60

↓20 Eternitie   Philip Pain, Daily Meditations (ed. Leon Howard, San
                        Marino, Calif., 1936), p. 9.

p.   60 continued

↑18 spirit   Hooker, Application of Redemption, p. 429.

↑ 7 it   Willard, Compleat Body, p. 266.

p.   61

↓ 3 be   Mitchell, Discourse of the Glory, pp. 113-114.

↓ 7 hopes   Hooker, Soules Exaltation, p. 123.

↓21 conversation   Hooker, Soules Vocation, pp. 390-391; cf. Cotton,
                         Way of Life, p. 431.

↑16 glorious   Cotton, A Practical Commentary . . . upon The First
                         Epistle Generall of John, p. 21.

↑13 discourage-   Cotton, Way of Life, p. 422.
     ments

↑ 8 vanity   Cotton, A Brief Exposition with Practicall Observations
                         upon The Whole Book of Ecclesiastes (London, 1654), p. 200.

↑ 1 mischiefe   Ibid., p. 119.

p.   62

↓ 8 grace   Shepard, Works, I, 329.

↓15 beloved   Hooker, Application of Redemption, pp. 137-138.

↑15 affected   Hooker, Soules Vocation, p. 118.

↑ 9 food   Ball, Treatise of Faith, p. 37.

↑ 4* off   Shepard, Preface to George Phillips, A Reply to a
                         Confutation of some grounds for Infants Baptisme
                         (London, 1645), p. A3 verso.

Chapter III: The Intellectual Character

p.   65

↓10* achieve it   Increase Mather, Two Plain and Practical Dis-
                   courses Concerning Hardness of Heart (London,
                   1699), p. 128; cf. Thomas Hooker, "The Poore
                   Doubting Christian," in The Saints Cordials
                   (London, 1629), p. 354.

↓12 fatal   Samuel Willard, Useful Instructions for a professing
                   People (Cambridge, 1673), p. 54.

↓14 putrefaction John Cotton, A Brief Exposition Of the whole Book of
                   Canticles (London, 1642), p. 96.

↓17 them   Willard, A Compleat Body of Divinity (1726), p. 35.

↓21 reason   Charles Chauncy, The Plain Doctrin of the Justification
                   of a Sinner in the sight of God (London, 1659),
                   p. 154.

p.   66

↓15 conception   Jonathan Mitchell, A Discourse of the Glory To which
                   God hath called Believers by Jesus Christ (London,
                   1677), p. 38.

↑21 actions   Robert Harris, "A Treatise of the New Covenant," in
                   Works (London, 1654), p. 3.

↑17 heaven   Mitchell, Discourse of the Glory, p. 37.

↑13 them   John Preston, Life Eternall (London, 1634), pt. I,
                   p. 63.

p.   67

↓ 1 them   Willard, Compleat Body, p. 592 (sig.**Gggl verso).

↓ 6 Willard   Ibid., p. 28.

↓ 9 Knowledge   Ibid., p. 12.

↓10 colors   Cotton, The way of Life (London, 1641), p. 178.

↓12 knowledge   Cotton, Christ the Fountaine of Life (London, 1651),
                   p. 145.

p.   67 continued

↓13   knowledge   Cotton, Way of Life, p. 177.

↓16* gifted   George Phillips, A Reply to a Confutation of some
                        grounds for Infants Baptisme (London, 1645), p. 119.

↓19   Events   Willard, The Heart Garrisoned (Cambridge, 1676),
                        p. 13.

↑18   know   John Norton, The Orthodox Evangelist (London, 1654),
                        Epistle Dedicatory.

↑14   faith   Hooker, The Soules Vocation (London, 1638), p. 287.

↑10   knowledge   Preston, The New Covenant (London, 1629), p. 446.

↑ 9   be   John Ball, A Treatise of Faith (London, 1632), p. 3.

↑ 6   requireth   Preston, Sinnes Overthrow (London, 1635), p. 26.

p.   68

↓20   respect   Urian Oakes, New-England Pleaded with (Cambridge,
                        1673), p. 10.

↑18* revealed   John Owen, Animadversions on a Treatise Intituled
                        Fiat Lux (London, 1662), p. 191.

↑13   Gospel   Joseph Sedgwick, A Sermon Preached at St. Marie's
                        (London, 1653), p. 20.

↑ 8* do   Willard, The Christians Exercise by Satans Temptations
                        (1701), p. 115.

↑ 5   things   Oakes, New-England Pleaded with, pp. 4-5.

↑ 3   conceptions   Thomas Bridge, Jethro's Advice (1710), p. 7.

p.   69

↓15   gainsaying   Hooker, A Survey of the Summe of Church-Discipline
                        (London, 1648), pt. I, p. 50.

↓17   interpretation Hooker, A Comment upon Christ's last Prayer (London,
                        1656), pp. 167-168.

p.   69 continued

↓19   reason   Hooker, <u>Survey</u>, p. C3 recto.

↓20   Councellour   William Hubbard, <u>The Happiness of a People in the</u> <u>Wisdome of their Rulers Directing</u> (1676), p. 32.

↑20   selves   Willard, <u>The Fiery Tryal no strange thing</u> (1682), p. A2 recto.

↑10   knowledge   John Hall, <u>An Humble Motion to The Parliament of</u> <u>England Concerning The Advancement of Learning</u> (London, 1649), p. 15.

p.   71

↓21   us   Cotton Mather, <u>A Companion for Communicants</u> (1690), pp. 10-11.

p.   72

↓15* things   Owen, <u>Animadversions on a Treatise Intituled Fiat</u> <u>Lux</u>, p. 192.

p.   73

↓ 2* make   Richard Baxter, <u>The Judgment of Non-Conformists of the</u> <u>interest of Reason in matters of Religion</u> (London, 1676), pp. 12-13.

↓15* <u>rational</u>   Ibid., pp. 8-9.

↑11   <u>Spirit</u>   William Dell, <u>A Plain and Necessary Confutation of</u> <u>Divers Gross and Anti-Christian Errors, Delivered to</u> <u>the University Congregation . . . by Mr. Sydrach</u> <u>Simpson</u> (London, 1654), p. 37.

p.   74

↑16   helpes   Thomas Hall, <u>Vindiciae Literarum</u> (London, 1655), pp. A3 recto - A3 verso.

↑ 3   Scripture   Edward Johnson, <u>Wonder-Working Providence</u> (ed. J. Franklin Jameson, New York, 1910), p. 127.

p.　75

↓ 7　not　　　　　John Webster, The Saints Guide (London, 1654),
　　　　　　　　　p. A3 recto.

↑ 5　Dust　　　　"New Englands First Fruits," in Samuel Eliot Morison,
　　　　　　　　　The Founding of Harvard College (Cambridge, 1935),
　　　　　　　　　p. 432.

p.　76

↓ 1　preaching　Ibid., pp. 248-250.

p.　78

↓ 7　ministry　　Dell, Plain and Necessary Confutation, p. A2 verso.

↓13　Christ　　　Webster, Saints Guide, pp. 1-2.

↓19　born　　　　Dell, The Tryal of Spirits (London, 1653), p. 54.

↑16　Gospel　　　Dell, Plain and Necessary Confutation, p. 39.

↑ 8　Poets　　　　Dell, Tryal of Spirits, p. 55.

↑ 5　Popery　　　Dell, Plain and Necessary Confutation, p. a3 recto.

p.　79

↓ 5　Canaan　　　Webster, Academiarum Examen (London, 1654), p. 8.

↓ 9　sake　　　　Dell, Tryal of Spirits, p. 51.

↓17　of　　　　　Dell, Plain and Necessary Confutation, p. 23.

↑ 9　Ministry　　Webster, Saints Guide, pp. 23-28.

p.　80

↓18　absence　　Dell, Plain and Necessary Confutation, p. 35.

↓22　them　　　　Dell, Tryal of Spirits, p. 50.

↑18　universities　Ibid., p. 43.

p.   80 continued

↑14 please   Ibid., p. 6.

↑10 Reason   Webster, Saints Guide, p. A2 recto.

p.   81

↓ 5 Art   Dell, Tryal of Spirits, p. 31.

↓ 7 for us   Cotton, The New Covenant (London, 1654), p. 10.

↓11 mind   Dell, Tryal of Spirits, p. 20.

↑12 others   Seth Ward, Vindiciae Academiarum (Oxford, 1654), p. 3.

↑ 3 alone   Dell, The Stumbling-Stone (London, 1653), pp. 27-28.

p.   82

↓ 1 it   Webster, Academiarum Examen, p. 3.

↓11 undervalued   Edward Reynolds, A Sermon Touching the Use of Humane
                     Learning (London, 1658), p. 12.

↑19 emulation   Ibid., p. 17.

↑15 Scripture   Ibid., pp. 18-19.

↑ 6 Learning   Ibid., pp. 22-23.

↑ 4 Christianity   Sedgwick, A Sermon Preached at St. Marie's, p. 8.

p.   83

↓ 1 unbefriended   Edward Waterhouse, An humble Apologie for Learning
                     and Learned Men (London, 1653), p. 109; cf. pp. 91ff.

↓14 brain   Sedgwick, A Sermon Preached at St. Marie's, p. 6.

↓18 Truth   Reynolds, A Sermon Touching the Use of Humane Learning,
                     pp. 19-22.

↑13 truth   Sedgwick, A Sermon Preached at St. Marie's, pp. 24-25.

p.   84

↓ 4* Soul   Sedgwick, <u>Learning's Necessity to an Able Minister</u>
                     <u>of the Gospel</u> (London, 1653), p. 56.

↓ 8 it   Reynolds, <u>A Sermon Touching the Use of Humane Learning</u>,
                     pp. 15-16.

↓17 same   <u>Records of the Governor and Company of Massachusetts</u>
                     <u>Bay in New England</u> (ed. N. B. Shurtleff, 1853-1854),
                     III, 279.

↑18* wilderness   Thomas Shepard, Jr., <u>Eye-Salve</u> (Cambridge, 1673),
                     p. 11.

↑15 together   Increase Mather, <u>A Discourse Concerning the Danger</u>
                     <u>of Apostacy</u> (2 ed., 1685), p. 101.

↑ 8 truth   Morison, <u>Founding of Harvard College</u>, p. 250.

↑ 1* Place   Peter Folger, <u>A Looking Glass for the Times</u> (Rhode
                     Island Historical Tracts No. 16, Providence, 1883),
                     pp. 14-15.

p.   85

↓17* Philosophy   Chauncy, <u>Gods Mercy, Shewed to his People</u> (Cambridge,
                     1655), p. 54.

↓21* Scriptures   <u>Ibid</u>., pp. 41-42.

↑15* hearers   <u>Ibid</u>., p. 52.

↑10* <u>Philosophy</u>   <u>Ibid</u>.

p.   86

↓16*˙ cheape   William Perkins, <u>Works</u>, I (London, 1626), Preface.

↓20 them   Hooker, <u>The Soules Preparation for Christ</u> (London,
                     1638), p. 70.

↑19 Religion   Hooker, <u>The Saints Dignitie, and Dutie</u> (London,
                     1651), p. 196.

p.   86 continued

↑13   disease   Hooker, <u>The Application of Redemption</u> (London, 1659),
                       pp. 88-90.

p.   87

↓10   Scriptures   John Dunton, <u>Letters written from New-England</u>
                       (The Prince Society, Boston, 1867), p. 26.

↑20   opinions   John Winthrop, <u>Winthrop's Journal, "History of New
                       England,"</u> 1630-1649 (ed. J. K. Hosmer, New York
                       1908), I, 209.

Chapter IV: The Intellectual Heritage

p.   93

↓ 3   Popery   John Cotton, <u>A Brief Exposition Of the whole</u>
                    <u>Book of Canticles</u> (London, 1642), p. 177.

↑21   way   Cotton, <u>The Way of Congregational Churches Cleared</u>
                    (London, 1648), pt. 1, p. 31.

↑20   divines   James Fitch, <u>Peace The End of the Perfect and Upright</u>
                    (Cambridge, 1672), p. 1.

↑16   Scripture   Thomas Hooker, <u>A Comment upon Christ's last Prayer</u>
                    (London, 1656), p. 157.

↑14   question   John Norton, <u>A Discussion of that Great Point in</u>
                    <u>Divinity, the Sufferings of Christ</u> (London, 1653),
                    p. 81.

↑ 3   errors   Norton, <u>The Heart of N-England rent at the Blasphemies</u>
                    <u>of the Present Generation</u> (Cambridge, 1659), p. 28.

p.   94

↑ 6   Church   William Ames, <u>Conscience with the Power and Cases</u>
                    <u>Thereof</u> (London, 1643), p. A2 verso.

p.   95

↓19   learning   Thomas Hall, <u>Vindiciae Literarum</u> (London, 1655), p. 15.

↑11   impression   Richard Baxter, <u>The Reasons of the Christian Religion</u>
                    (London, 1667), pp. a3 recto - a3 verso.

↑ 8   sermons   Samuel Clarke, <u>A Generall Martyrologie</u> (London, 1651),
                    p. 483.

↑4   sermons   Samuel Willard, <u>A Compleat Body of Divinity</u> (1726), p. 1.

p.   96

↓21   perfect   John Wollebius, <u>The Abridgment of Christian Divinity</u>
                    (tr. Alexander Ross, 3 ed., London, 1660), p. A3 verso.

p.   97

↓ 1*   itself   Petro van Mastricht, Theoretico-Practica Theologia
                     (1699), p. 3.

↑21*   it   Augustine, On Christian Doctrine, bk. II, §60-61.

↑19*   in hand   Joseph Sedgwick, Learning's Necessity to an Able
                     Minister of the Gospel (London, 1653), p. 43.

↑10   since   Cotton Mather, American Tears upon the Ruines of the
                     Greek Churches (1701), pp. 42-43.

p.   98

↓ 2   Dunster   "The Winthrop Papers," IV Collections of the Massachu-
                     setts Historical Society, vii, 272.

↓ 4   truths   Samuel Eliot Morison, Harvard College in the Seventeenth
                     Century (Cambridge, 1936), p. 145.

↓10*   writ   Charles Chauncy, Gods Mercy, Shewed to his People
                     (Cambridge, 1655), p. 36.

↓13*   usum   Ibid., pp. 36-37.

↓15   together   Increase Mather, A Discourse Concerning the Danger of
                     Apostacy (2 ed., 1685), p. 101.

↓20   train   Cotton Mather, Corderius Americanus (1708), p. 29.

↑17   Evangelical   Cotton, A Briefe Exposition with Practicall Observations
                     upon The Whole Book of Ecclesiastes (London, 1654),
                     p. 129.

↑ 7   Conversation Increase Mather, Wo to Drunkards (Cambridge, 1673), p. 15

↑ 2*   Sinful   Increase Mather, An Arrow against Profane and Promiscuous
                     Dancing (1684), p. 16; cf. also Some Important Truths
                     Concerning Conversion (2 ed., 1684), p. 90.

p.   99

↓19   communities   William Hubbard, The Benefit of a Well-Ordered
                     Conversation (1684), p. 66.

p. 99 continued

↑19 Interpreter   Increase Mather, Preface to Samuel Mather, <u>A
                    Testimony from the Scripture against Idolatry &
                    Superstition</u> (Cambridge, 1670), p. A3 verso.

↑18 produced   Increase Mather, <u>A Discourse Concerning the Uncertainty
                    of the Times of Men</u> (1697), p. 37.

↑12 writings   Increase Mather, <u>An Essay for the Recording of Illus-
                    trious Providences</u> [1684] (ed. George Offor, as
                    <u>Remarkable Providences</u>, London, 1856), p. 241.

↑10 <u>Philosophers</u>   Hubbard, <u>Benefit of a Well-Ordered Conversation</u>, p. 14.

p. 100

↓ 7 errors   Thomas Hall, <u>Vindiciae Litcrarum</u>, p. 51; Richard
                    Bernard, <u>The Faithfull Shepherd</u> (London, 1621), p. 157.

↓13 nauseousness   John Webster, <u>Academiarum Examen</u> (London, 1654), p. 15.

↓21 Latine   Cotton, <u>An Exposition upon The Thirteenth Chapter of
                    the Revelation</u> (London, 1656), p. 27.

p. 101

↓ 1 Popery   <u>Ibid.</u>, p. 23.

↓11* Occam   Cf. Richard Sibbes, <u>Works</u> (ed. Alexander B. Grosart,
                    Edinburgh, 1862-64), I, lxxxiv.

↑11 fatnesse   John Preston, <u>Life Eternall</u> (London, 1634), pp. A6
                    verso - A7 recto.

p. 102

↓ 1 kinde   Hooker, <u>The Soules Exaltation</u> (London, 1638), p. 36.

p. 104

↓17 off   Clarke, <u>A Generall Martyrologie</u>, p. 478.

↑13 done   Cotton, Preface to John Norton, <u>The Orthodox Evangelist</u>
                    (London, 1654).

p. 104 continued

↑ 9 objection   Cotton, A Practical Commentary . . . upon The First
                  Epistle Generall of John (London, 1656), p. 132.

↑ 5 admirable   Hooker, A Survey of the Summe of Church-Discipline
                  (London, 1648), pt. I, p. 96.

↑ 1 another   Ibid., pt. I, p. 66; The Christians Two Chiefe Lessons
                  (London, 1640), p. 295.

p. 105

↓ 3 it   John Davenport, Preface to Henry Scudder, The Christians
                  Daily Walke (London, 1635), p. A4 Verso; cf. The Saints
                  Anchor-Hold (London, 1661), p. 175.

↓ 6* Victoire   Increase Mather, Diatriba de Signo Filii Hominis
                  (Amsterdam, 1682), passim.

↓10 distinctions Samuel Lee, The Joy of Faith (1687), p. 70.

↓15* extremes   Van Mastricht, Theoretico-Practica Theologia, p. 3.

↑21 form   Hooker, Survey, pt. I, p. 91.

↑ 3* precepts   Chauncy, Gods Mercy, Shewed to his People, p. 37.

p. 106

↓ 8 arts   Theses technologicae, Nos. 2, 5, 1670; No. 5, 1678;
                  No. 2, 1689.

↓ 9 donum   Magirus, Physiologiae Peripateticae (Geneva, 1638),
                  p. A2 recto.

↓15* Science   John Richardson, The Necessity of a Well Experienced
                  Souldiery (Cambridge, 1679), p. 9.

↑21* Ghost   Bartholomäus Keckermann, Operum Omnium Quae Extant
                  (Geneva, 1614), I, 18-19.

↑16* ordered   Ames, Philosophemata (Leyden, 1643), p. 14.

↑ 6 Imagination Charles Morton, The Spirit of Man (1693), pp. 21-22.

p.   107

↓ 3   vinculo   Theses technologicae, No. 6, 1691; No. 7, 1719.

↓ 4   the arts   Theses technologicae, No. 4, 1691.

↓ 5   God   Theses technologicae, No. 4, 1670.

↓16   Ends   Willard, Compleat Body, p. 3.

↑21* salvation   Johann Heinrich Alsted, Encyclopaedia (1649), I, 69.

Chapter V: The Instrument of Reason

p. 111

↓ 5   twisted   Marcus Fredericus Wendelin, Logicae Institutiones
                       (Amsterdam, 1654), p. *4 recto.

p. 112

↓ 8   truthe   Thomas Wilson, The Rule of Reason (London, 1552),
                       p. 2 verso.

↓18* intelligence   Frederic Beurhusius, De P. Rami Dialecticae prae-
                       cipuis capitibus disputationes scholasticae (1682),
                       pp. A2 recto - A3 verso.

↓21   judgement   Thomas Spencer, The Art of Logick (London, 1628),
                       p. A3 recto; cf. Wendelin, Logicae Institutiones,
                       p. *4 recto.

↑ 1   fallacies   Theses logicae, No. 17, 1653 (Aug. 10).

p. 113

↓10* assiduously   Bartholomäus Keckermann, Operum Omnium Quae Extant
                       (Geneva, 1614), I, 110.

↓20* philosopher   Johann Heinrich Alsted, Encyclopaedia (1649), I, 102.

↑18* seductores   Conrad Dietrich, Institutiones Dialecticae (1655),
                       p. 9.

↑15* arts   Cornelius Martin, Commentariorum Logicorum adversus
                       Ramistas (1623), pp. 1, 2.

↑ 8* logic   William Rodingus, ed., Ramus' Dialecticae Libri Duo
                       (Frankfort, 1579), pp. 3-4.

↑ 4   respects   Henry Diest, De Ratione Studii Theologici (Amsterdam,
                       1624), pp. 15-16.

p. 114

↓ 4   not   Richard Bernard, The Faithfull Shepherd (London,
                       1621), pp. 49-50.

↓16   game   John Webster, Academiarum Examen (London, 1654),
                       pp. 14-16.

p. 114 continued

↑16* Scripture   Charles Chauncy, Gods Mercy, Shewed to his People
                        (Cambridge, 1655), p. 48.

↑13 Reason   John Eliot, The Logic Primer [Cambridge, 1672] (ed.
                        Wilberforce Eames, Cleveland, 1904), title page.

↑10* conclusions   John Davenport, The Saints Anchor-Hold (London, 1661).
                        p. 61.

↑ 7 in it   Samuel Willard, Brief Directions to a Young Scholar
                        Designing the Ministry, for the Study of Divinity
                        (1735), p. 2.

↑ 2* them   Willard, Heavenly Merchandize (1686), pp. 111-112.

p. 115

↓14 light   Samuel Mather, Preface to Samuel Stone, A Congrega-
                        tional Church is a Catholike Visible Church (London,
                        1652), p. A2 recto.

↑ 3 Logick   Webster, Academiarum Examen, p. 91.

p. 117

↑14* doctrine   Ramus, Dialectique (1576), Preface.

p. 118

↑18 master   Samuel Eliot Morison, Harvard College in the Seven-
                        teenth Century (Cambridge, 1936), pp. 167-168.

↑ 8 Bacon   Cotton Mather, Magnalia Christi Americana (Hartford,
                        1853-55), II, 21.

p. 119

↓10 advantage   Increase Mather, Preface to James Fitch, The first
                        Principles of the Doctrine of Christ (1679), pp. A2
                        verso - A3 recto.

p. 120

↓10 indeed   Morison, <u>Harvard College in the Seventeenth Century</u>,
                          p. 640.

↑ 3 Government   Increase Mather, <u>A Discourse Concerning the Danger</u>
                          <u>of Apostacy</u> (2 ed., 1685), p. 125; Cotton Mather,
                          <u>A Letter of Advice to the Churches of the Non-conform-</u>
                          <u>ists in the English Nation</u> (London, 1700), p. 1.

p. 121

↓ 3 it   Samuel Stone, <u>A Congregational Church is a Catholike</u>
                          <u>Visible Church</u>, p. F2 verso.

↓16 doctissime   Cotton Mather, <u>Parentator</u> (1724), pp. 14-15.

↑ 6 Aristotelian   Theses technologicae, No. 27, 1719.

p. 123

↓21* service   Charles Waddington, <u>Ramus, sa vie, ses écrits et</u>
                          <u>ses opinions</u> (Paris, 1855), pp. 23-24.

p. 124

↓ 4* else   Ramus, <u>Dialecticae Libri Duo</u> (1574), p. 5.

↓22 coincidunt   Samuel Johnson (ed. Herbert and Carol Schneider, New
                          York, 1929), II, 70.

↑19* concluding   Abraham Fraunce, <u>The Lawiers Logike</u> (London, 1588),
                          p. 9 verso.

↑13* conception   Ramus, <u>Dialectique</u>, pp. 3-4.

↑ 6 parallel   Theses logicae, No. 2, 1653 (Aug. 10); No. 3, 1670.

↑ 2* verbs   Joachimus Perionius, <u>De Dialectica</u> (1544), p. 441.

p. 125

↓ 3* you   Nicodemus Frischlin, <u>Contra P. Rami</u> (Frankfort, 1590),
                          pp. 4-5.

p. 125 continued

↓ 4* unreliable Ramus, <u>Scholarum Dialecticarum</u> (Frankfort, 1581), pp. 73ff.

↓12* respect William Brattle, MS <u>Compendium of Logick</u> (copied by Nathan Prince; Massachusetts Historical Society), pt. I, ch. 2.

↓ 14 truth Theses logicae, No. 12, 1719.

↓19* art Ramus, <u>Scholarum Dialecticarum</u>, p. 112.

↑21 method Alexander Richardson, <u>The Logicians School-Master</u> (London, 1657), p. 71.

↑17* order Henningus Rennemannus, <u>Dissertatio pro Philosophia Ramea, adversus Peripateticas</u> (Frankfort, 1595), p. 26.

↑ 9 dispute John Hall, <u>An Humble Motion to The Parliament of England Concerning The Advancement of Learning</u> (London, 1649), p. 38.

p. 127

↓ 1 asunder Richardson, <u>Logicians School-Master</u>, p. 38.

↓ 4* disserere Fraunce, <u>Lawiers Logike</u>, pp. 2 verso - 3 recto.

↓ 6 England Theses technologicae, No. 5, 1689.

↑ 4* man Christopher Marlowe, <u>Plays</u> (Everyman's Library Edition), p. 306.

p. 128

↓ 9 Creatures Richardson, <u>Logicians School-Master</u>, pp. 36-37.

↓10 well Willard, <u>A Brief Reply to Mr. George Kieth</u> (1703), p. 47.

↑21* cognition Ramus, <u>Institutionum Dialecticarum</u> (Paris, 1552), pp. 187-188.

↑20 1643 Theses logicae, No. 1, 1643.

p. 128 continued

↑ 9 gemelli   Theses logicae, No. 2, 1687; No. 2, 1670.

p. 129

↓ 3 together   Richardson, Logicians School-Master, pp. 54, 56.

↓ 5* forth   George Downame, Commentarii in P. Rami Regii
                     Professoris, Dialecticam (London, 1669), p. 8.

↓11 any   Stone, A Congregational Church is a Catholike Visible
                     Church, p. D4 verso.

↓14 Logick   Samuel Mather, Preface to Stone, A Congregational
                     Church is a Catholike Visible Church.

↓21* arguments   Ramus, Scholarum Dialecticarum, p. 102.

↓22* modo   Rennemannus, Dissertatio, p. 64.

↑12 it   Richardson, Logicians School-Master, p. 69.

↑ 8 eye   Ibid.

↑ 3 inartificiale   Ibid., pp. 75-76.

p. 130

↓ 2 truth   Stone, A Congregational Church is a Catholike Visible
                     Church, p. F3 recto.

↓ 5 artificials   Richardson, Logicians School-Master, p. 233.

↓18* so   Anthony Wotton, The Art of Logick (London, 1626),
                     p. 108.

↑17* die   Marlowe, Plays (Everyman's Library Edition), p. 306.

↑13* dependeth   Wotton, Art of Logick, pp. 107-108.

↑ 6*(2)Reasoning   James Fitch, First Principles, pp. 57-59; An
                     Explanation of the Solemn Advice (1683), p. 81.

p. 131

↓18* etc.   Sir William Temple, ed., Ramus' Dialecticae (Cambridge, Eng., 1584), p. 63.

↑16 glue   Richardson, Logicians School-Master, pp. 65ff.

↑ 9* proposed   Rennemannus, Dissertatio, p. 34.

p. 132

↓18* Method   Wotton, Art of Logick, p. 114.

↑13 method   John Cotton, A Briefe Exposition with Practicall Observations upon The Whole Book of Ecclesiastes (London, 1654), p. 265.

p. 133

↓15* disposition Henry Schorus, Specimen et forma legitime tradendi sermonis (1572), pp. 38-39.

↓19 really   Theses logicae, No. 18, 1647.

↑ 5* judgment   Ramus, Dialectique, p. 55.

p. 134

↓14* art   Ramus, Institutionum Dialecticarum, p. 132.

↑20* sentence   Ibid., p. 130.

↑ 3* syllogismes Fraunce, Lawiers Logike, p. 98 recto.

p. 135

↑14 axioms   Richardson, Logicians School-Master, pp. 51, 334-335, 293-295.

↑12* axiom   William Ames, Philosophemata (Leyden, 1643), p. 225.

↑ 6* syllogism   Ibid., p. 179.

↑ 4 syllogism   Theses logicae, No. 14, 1647; No. 23, 1678.

p. 136

↑19* Aristotle   Piscator, ed., <u>P. Rami Dialecticae Libri Duo. . .</u>
                        (Frankfort, 1583), pp. 307-308, 322-323.

↑10* than the   Downame, <u>Commentarii</u>, p. 448.
     simple

↑ 4 Logician   Richardson, <u>Logicians School-Master</u>, pp. 328, 307.

p. 137

↑16* arguments   Downame, <u>Commentarii</u>, p. 129.

↑13 confirmed   Spencer, <u>Art of Logick</u>, p. 169. (Incorrect).

↑10 Logick   Richardson, <u>Logicians School-Master</u>, pp. 150-151.

↑ 6 denied   Theses logicae, No. 6, 1643.

↑ 4 perpetual   Theses logicae, No. 8, 1646.

p. 138

↓ 4 distinguish   Theses logicae, No. 22, 1678.

↓ 7 another   Richardson, <u>Logicians School-Master</u>, pp. 325-329.

↓ 9* false   Ames, <u>Philosophemata</u>, p. 229.

↓13 axiome   Quoted in William Twisse, <u>A Treatise of Mr. Cottons</u>
                        <u>Clearing certaine Doubts Concerning Predestination.</u>
                        <u>Together with an examination thereof</u> (London, 1646),
                        p. 100.

↓16 himself   Fitch, <u>First Principles</u>, p. 59.

↓18 Time   Willard, <u>A Compleat Body of Divinity</u> (1726), p. 108.

↑19* contradiction   Willard, <u>A Brief Discourse of Justification</u> (1686),
                        p. 65.

↑17* Disjunctive   Willard, <u>The Best Priviledge</u> (1701), p. 2.

↑14* true   Willard, <u>Heavenly Merchandize</u>, pp. 113-114.

p. 138 continued

↑ 9 destroyed   Willard, <u>Brief Directions to a Young Scholar</u>, p. 4.

p. 139

↓ 3 method   Richardson, <u>Logicians School-Master</u>, p. 341.

↓ 7* syllogism   Ramus, <u>Dialectique</u>, p. 57.

↓10* port   Ramus, <u>Institutionum Dialecticarum</u>, pp. 143-144.

↓20* judgment   Ramus, <u>Dialectique</u>, pp. 64-65.

↑17 Art   Increase Mather, Preface to Fitch, <u>First Principles</u>,
                     pp. A2 verso - A3 recto.

↑14 confusion   <u>Theses logicae</u>, No. 18, 1653 (Aug. 10); Willard,
                     <u>Compleat Body</u>, p. 26.

↑ 5* arrangement   Ramus, <u>Dialectique</u>, p. 58.

↑ 2* them   Fraunce, <u>Lawiers Logike</u>, p. 6 recto.

p. 140

↓ 1 invented   Theses logicae, No. 20, 1687.

↓ 7* prolixity   Arnaud de Ossat, <u>Expositio in Disputationem</u> (Paris,
                     1564), p. 2.

↓15 thesis   Theses logicae, No. 17, 1653 (Aug. 9).

↓19* afterwards   Ramus, <u>Dialectique</u>, p. 56.

↓21 singulars   Theses logicae, No. 13, 1643.

↑18* whole   Ramus, <u>Dialectique</u>, p. 57.

↑ 6 method   Richardson, <u>Logicians School-Master</u>, pp. 338-339.

↑ 3 continually   <u>Ibid</u>., p. 336.

↑ 1 doth   John Eliot, <u>The Logic Primer</u>, pp. 74-76.

p. 141

↓11* later   Fraunce, <u>Lawiers Logike</u>, pp. 87 verso - 88 recto.

↓14* reciprocal   Ramus, <u>Scholarum Dialecticarum</u>, p. 32.

↓21 knowledge   Ames, <u>Philosophemata</u>, pp. 14, 24, 173.

↓23 formed   Theses logicas, No. 12, 1642.

p. 142

↓ 1* logic   Frank P. Graves, <u>Peter Ramus and the Educational Reforma</u>
                    <u>tion of the Sixteenth Century</u> (New York, 1912), p. 21.

↓ 3* usage   <u>Ibid</u>., pp. 29-30.

↓ 4* exercise   Ramus, <u>Institutionum Dialecticarum</u>, p. 146.

↓13* them   Ramus, <u>Dialectique</u>, pp. 65-67.

↓21 extant   <u>The Logicke of the Most Excellent Philosopher P. Ramus</u>
                    <u>Martyr</u> (London, 1574), pp. 14, 15.

↑20* capacities   Robert Fage, <u>Peter Ramus . . . his Dialectica in two</u>
                    <u>books</u> (London, 1632), Preface.

↑19 use   Theses logicae, No. 1, 1647; No. 5, 1646.

↑17* usuarius   Graves, <u>Peter Ramus</u>, p. 57.

p. 143

↓13* none   Fraunce, <u>Lawiers Logike</u>, pp. 2 verso - 3 recto.

↓18* things   Rennemannus, <u>Dissertatio</u>, p. 56; cf. pp. 63-79;
                    Wendelin, <u>Logicae Institutiones</u>, pp. **1 ff.

↑11* sordidae   Rennemannus, <u>Dissertatio</u>, p. 26.

↑ 2* nature   Waddington, <u>Ramus</u>, pp. 354-355; p. 374.

p. 144

↓ 1 things   Theses logicae, No. 1, 1646.

p. 144 continued

↓ 6* it   Rennemannus, Dissertatio, p. 119.

↓18 things   Theses logicae, No. 1, 1670.

↑15* men   Ramus, Scholarum Dialecticarum, p. 33.

↑14 people   Richardson, Logicians School-Master, p. 233.

↑ 8* art   Waddington, Ramus, p. 368.

↑ 1* inuented   Fraunce, Lawiers Logike, p. 2 recto.

p. 145

↓ 2 mind   Theses logicae, No. 1, 1689.

↓ 7* imperfection   Fraunce, Lawiers Logike, p. 2 recto.

↓10* drawe   Ibid., p. 2 verso.

↓14* bewilderment   Sir William Temple, Pro Mildapetti de Vnica Methodo
                      Defensione contra Diplodophilum . . . (Frankfort,
                      1584), pp. 107-112.

↓16* lives   Gosivino Mulhemius, Logica ad P. Rami Dialecticam
                      Conformata (Frankfort, 1584), p. A3 verso.

↑19* autors   Fraunce, Lawiers Logike, p. 2 recto.

↑ 8* it   Ramus, Dialecticae Libri Duo, p. 15.

p. 146

↓ 2* artificiall   Fraunce, Lawiers Logike, p. 3 verso.

↓17* eagerness   Ramus, Commentariorum de Religione Christiana
                      (Frankfort, 1577), pp. 1-5 and passim; Waddington,
                      Ramus, pp. 360-361.

↑10* reason   Adrien Heereboord, Meletemata Philosophica
                      (Leyden, 1659), p. 1.

↑ 6* foundations   Rennemannus, Dissertatio, p. 27.

p. 147

↓ 3* disputed   Sir William Temple, <u>Epistolae de P. Rami Dialectica</u> (Cambridge, Eng., 1684), p. 250; cf. p. 264.

↓12   them   Richardson, <u>Logicians School-Master</u>, p. 219.

↓15* it   Wotton, <u>Art of Logick</u>, p. 120.

↓20   axioms   Theses logicae, No. 2, 1646; No. 2, 1647; No. 21, 1687.

↑ 4   not   Stone, <u>A Congregational Church is a Catholike Visible Church</u>, p. C1 verso.

p. 148

↓10   him   <u>Ibid</u>., p. D2 verso.

↓12   them   <u>Ibid</u>., p. D3 verso.

↓14   thing   <u>Ibid</u>., p. D4 verso.

↑ 7   thesis   Theses logicae, No. 4, 1687.

p. 149

↓ 6* thing   Wotton, <u>Art of Logick</u>, p. 4.

↓19* Ames   Ames, <u>Philosophemata</u>, p. 21.

↑17   livery   Stone, <u>A Congregational Church is a Catholike Visible Church</u>, p. C4 verso.

p. 150

↓ 6   disposed   Richardson, <u>Logicians School-Master</u>, pp. 46ff.

↓ 9   things   Theses logicae, No. 2, 1678; No. 3, 1687.

↓18* things   Ames, <u>Philosophemata</u>, p. 195.

↓22* things   <u>Ibid</u>., p. 217.

↑20* nature   <u>Ibid</u>., p. 230.

↑18* themselves   <u>Ibid</u>., p. 196.

p. 150 continued

↑12* itself   Ibid.

p. 151

↓12* eye   Fraunce, Lawiers Logike, p. 4 verso.

↓15* nature   Mulhemius, Logica ad P. Rami Dialecticam Conformata,
                    p. A2 verso.

↓18 nerve   Mock theses logicae, No. 1, 1663.

↑19 thing   Richardson, Logicians School-Master, p. 262.

↑ 5* authority   Waddington, Ramus, p. 343n.

p. 152

↓ 5* Aristotelians Graves, Peter Ramus, p. 27.

↑19* state   Ursinus, Organi Aristotelei (1586), Preface.

p. 153

↑ 7* order   Downame, Commentarii, p. 5.

Chapter VI: Knowledge

↓ 2* them   Ramus, <u>Dialectique</u> (1576), pp. 37-38.

↓ 7* it   <u>Ibid</u>., pp. 1-2.

p. 160

↓ 4* Him   Frederic Beurhusius, <u>In P. Rami . . . Dialecticae</u>
                     (London, 1581), pp. 4-14.

↑20 Sciences   Alexander Richardson, <u>The Logicians School-Master</u>
                     (London, 1657), pp. A3 recto - A4 recto.

↑17 God   <u>Ibid</u>., p. 82.

↑10 thereof   <u>Ibid</u>., p. 17.

↑ 5 <u>Encyclopaedia</u>   <u>Ibid</u>., p. 343.

p. 161

↓ 4* prescribed   William Ames, <u>Philosophemata</u> (Leyden, 1643), Preface.

↑21 <u>Encuclopaidia</u>   Richardson, <u>Logicians School-Master</u>, p. 17.

p. 162

↑13 out   <u>Ibid</u>., pp. 48-49.

p. 163

↓20 us   <u>Ibid</u>., pp. 1, 4, 7, 21.

↑17 Reason   James Fitch, <u>The first Principles of the Doctrine of
                     Christ</u> (1679), p. 6.

↑13 comfortable   Samuel Willard, <u>A Compleat Body of Divinity</u> (1726),
                     p. 43.

↑ 6 shines   Richardson, <u>Logicians School-Master</u>, p. 7.

p. 164

↓ 5 night   Theses technologicae, No. 2, 1670.

-42-

p. 164 continued

↓ 6 wisdom   Mock theses technologicae, No. 1, 1663.

↓12 omega of the   Richardson, Logicians School-Master, p. 15.
   arts

↓18* here   Thomas Hooker, Heavens Treasury Opened (London, 1645).
          p. 33.

↓21 arts   Theses technologicae, No. 4, 1719; No. 1, 1708; No. 5,
          1678.

↑20 scope   Theses technologicae, No. 2, 1653 (Aug. 9).

↑19 technologia   Theses technologicae, No. 2, 1708.

↑12 end   Richardson, Logicians School-Master, p. 9.

↑10 end   Ibid., p. 25.

↑ 9 employed   Theses technologicae, No. 6, 1719.

↑ 8 thing   Theses technologicae, No. 4, 1708.

p. 165

↓ 2 eupraxia   Richardson, Logicians School-Master, pp. 21-22.

↓ 4 aim   Ibid., p. 5.

↑10* ectypal   Ames, Philosophemata, pp. 14, 70, 145-146; cf. Johann
          Heinrich Alsted, Encyclopaedia (1649), I, 61.

p. 166

↓ 5 formed   Theses technologicae, No. 13, 1678; No. 5, 1693.

↓ 5 arts   Theses technologicae, No. 9, 1691.

↓ 7 nature   Theses technologicae, No. 3, 1693.

↓ 9 nature   Mock theses technologicae, No. 7, 1663; cf. Nos. 5 and
          6, 1663.

↓16 thing   Richardson, Logicians School-Master, pp. 261-262.

p. 166 continued

↑20 thing   Ibid., p. 19.

↑11* work   Ames, Philosophemata, pp. 4, 58-59; cf. Thomas
                          Shepard, Jr., "My logicall and physicall synopses,"
                          (MS dated 1655 in the Massachusetts Historical
                          Society), pp. 1, 2.

↑ 6 made   Richardson, Logicians School-Master, p. 16.

↑ 3 thing   Ibid., p. 25.

p. 167

↓14 wisdom   Theses technologicae, No. 5, 1670; No. 2, 1689.

↓20 being   Theses technologicae, No. 5, 1719; Quaestiones, No. 2
                          1664.

↑17 themselves   Fitch, First Principles, p. 15.

↑11 in it   Willard, Compleat Body, p. 102.

↑ 5* Truths   Willard, Heavenly Merchandize (1686), p. 8.

↑ 1 just   Willard, Compleat Body, p. 149.

p. 168

↓15* discovered   Hooker, Heavens Treasury Opened, p. 32.

↓18 being   Theses technologicae, No. 1, 1653 (Aug. 10).

↓21 good   Theses technologicae, No. 4, 1653 (Aug. 9); No. 6,
                          1653 (Aug. 10).

↑11 understanding   Ames, The Marrow of Sacred Divinity (London, 1643),
                          pp. 24-25.

↑ 5 the mind   Richardson, Logicians School-Master, p. 41.

p. 169

↓ 3 glass   Ibid., pp. 22-23.

p. 169 continued

↓ 9 astonishing   Willard, Compleat Body, p. 67.

↓20 Time   Ibid., p. 108.

p. 170

↑18 skilfully   Ames, Marrow, p. 26.

↑ 8 cause   Theses technologicae, No. 2, 1653 (Aug. 10); No. 3,
                    1687.

↑ 3 differ   Theses technologicae, No. 10, 1691.

p. 171

↓ 3 Prudence   Theses technologicae, No. 1, 1678.

↓15* reason   Ames, Philosophemata, p. 146; cf. pp. 6-7, 12, 17, 63,
                    67, 71.

↑20 patterns   Samuel Stone, A Congregational Church is a Catholike
                    Visible Church (London, 1652), p. D3 recto; cf.
                    Richardson, Logicians School-Master, p. 18; Ames,
                    Marrow, p. 25.

↑14 themselves   Willard, Compleat Body, p. 50; cf. pp. 52-55.

↑ 6 governs   Theses technologicae, No. 7, 1670; cf. No. 5, 1653
                    (Aug. 9).

p. 172

↓ 1 all   Richardson, Logicians School-Master, p. 254.

↓ 8 end   Ibid., p. 20.

↓10 theses   Theses technologicae, No. 7, 1719; No. 6, 1691.

↓17* axioms   Ramus, Dialectique, p. 9.

↓18* arts   Henningus Rennemannus, Dissertatio pro Philosophia
                    Ramea, adversus Peripateticas (Frankfort, 1595),
                    p. 25.

↓21* antecedents   Ames, Philosophemata, pp. 3, 14, 56, 69.

p. 172 continued

↓23 precepts   Theses logicae, No. 17, 1670; theses technologicae,
                       No. 1, 1693.

p. 173

↓ 1 light   Thomas Bridge, Jethro's Advice (1710), p. 7.

↓ 6 descend   Richardson, Logicians School-Master, "Notes of
                       Physicks," p. 96.

↓ 8 another   Stone, A Congregational Church is a Catholike Visible
                       Church, p. C3 recto.

↓12 world   Richardson, Logicians School-Master, "Notes of Physicks,
                       pp. 96-97.

↑19* eupraxia   Ames, Philosophemata, pp. 4-6, 59, 61, 145.

↑18 directed   Ames, Marrow, p. 2.

↑13 delineated   Theses technologicae, No. 5, 1708; No. 1, 1689; No. 2,
                       1691; No. 2, 1719; No. 10, 1719; No. 1, 1687.

↑ 8* out   Willard, Heavenly Merchandize, p. 112.

p. 174

↓ 9 doing   Richardson, Logicians School-Master, pp. 25ff.

↓13 1687   Theses technologicae, No. 8, 1687.

↑19 before   Richardson, Logicians School-Master, pp. 28-29.

↑15* Genesis   Ames, Philosophemata, p. 146.

↑ 8 Genesis   Theses technologicae, No. 6, 1687.

↑ 3 end   Theses technologicae, No. 8, 1678.

↑ 2 prattomenon   Theses technologicae, No. 7, 1687.

p. 175

↓ 4 prattomenon   Richardson, Logicians School-Master, p. 31.

p. 175 continued

↓10 πραττόμενον   Samuel Eliot Morison, Harvard College in the
                    Seventeenth Century (Cambridge, 1936), p. 278.

p. 176

↑ 5 Learning   Samuel Johnson (ed. Herbert and Carol Schneider, New
                    York, 1929), II, 186.

p. 177

↓15* it   Ames, Philosophemata, p. 5.

↑ 3* philosophers   Charles Waddington, Ramus, sa vie, ses écrits et ses
                    opinions (Paris, 1855), p. 403.

p. 178

↓ 4 judgment   Ibid., pp. 24-27.

↓ 7* conceptions   Francois Hotoman, Dialectica Institutiones (Geneva,
                    1573), pp. 11-12; cf. Rennemannus, Dissertatio,
                    pp. 99-100.

↓18 definition   Willard, Compleat Body, p. 41.

↑18 exist   Quaestiones, 1687.

↑17 words   Richardson, Logicians School-Master, p. 87.

p. 179

↑16 understood   Willard, Compleat Body, pp. 41-42.

↑13 ridiculous   Ibid., p. 592 (sig. *Gggl verso).

p. 180

↑14 flow   Samuel Mather, Preface to Stone, A Congregational
                    Church is a Catholike Visible Church, p. A2 recto.

Chapter VII: The Uses of Reason

p. 181

↑ 1 Capacities   Samuel Willard, A Compleat Body of Divinity (1726),
                         pp. 559-561.

p. 182

↓ 7 him   Ibid., p. 564.

↓10 Service   Ibid., p. 591 (sig. *Gggl recto).

↑ 6 Artist   Ibid., p. 10.

p. 183

↓ 2 vera   Alexander Richardson, The Logicians School-Master
                         (London, 1657), p. 13.

↓ 5 guilt   Cf. Willard, Compleat Body, pp. 7, 564.

↓13 Glory   Willard, The Heart Garrisoned (Cambridge, 1676), p. 10.

↓17 Himself   Urian Oakes, The Soveraign Efficacy of Divine Providenc
                         (1682), p. 6.

↑19 was   Richard Baxter, The Reasons of the Christian Religion
                         (London, 1667), p. 2-4.

↑16* way   Willard, Heavenly Merchandize (1686), p. 85.

↑ 4 it   John Cotton, A Briefe Exposition with Practicall Observ
                         tions upon The Whole Book of Ecclesiastes (London, 1654
                         pp. 162-163; John Preston, Life Eternall (London, 1634)
                         pp. 15-16; Willard, Compleat Body, pp. 493, 210.

p. 184

↓ 8* fall   William Perkins, Works, I (London, 1626), p. 637.

↓16 art   Theses logicae, No. 3, 1653 (Aug. 9); theses technologi
                         No. 3, 1653 (Aug. 10).

↑19 Conscience   Willard, Compleat Body, p. 36.

↑13 a man   Thomas Hooker, A Survey of the Summe of Church-Discipli
                         (London, 1648), pt. I, p. 44.

. 184 continued

9 naturall   Cotton, A Practical Commentary . . . upon The First
                  Epistle Generall of John (London, 1656), p. 8.

5 object   Samuel Eliot Morison, Harvard College in the Seventeenth
                  Century (Cambridge, 1936), p. 130.

2 altogether   Willard, Compleat Body, p. 40.

. 185

2 disband   Willard, The Christians Exercise by Satans Temptations
                  (1701), pp. 99-100.

8* all   Samuel Lee, The Great Day of Judgment (1692), pp. 5-6.

17 him   Willard, Compleat Body, pp. 754, 150.

19 mistaken   Ibid., pp. 15-16.

13* principles   Johann Heinrich Alsted, Encyclopaedia (1649), I, 51.

9 Nature   Willard, Compleat Body, p. 614 (sig. Eeeel verso).

6* done   Increase Mather, Two Plain and Practical Discourses
                  Concerning Hardness of Heart (London, 1699), pp. 88-89.

4* breast   Increase Mather, Wo to Drunkards (Cambridge, 1673),
                  p. 5.

2 Law   John Davenport, "A Sermon Preach'd at The Election of
                  the Governour at Boston in New-England, May 19th,
                  1669," p. 4, in Publications of the Colonial Society
                  of Massachusetts, X (1907).

. 186

7 these   Cotton, A Practical Commentary . . . upon The First
                  Epistle Generall of John, pp. 123-124.

21 frame   John Preston, Life Eternall, p. A7 recto.

13 them   Preston, The Saints Qualification (London, 1633),
                  pp. 128-129.

p. 187

↓ 9 ripeness   Hooker, <u>The Application of Redemption</u> (London, 1659), p. 142.

↓13 God   <u>Ibid.</u>, p. 369.

↓18 men   Increase Mather, <u>A Sermon Occasioned by the Execution of a Man found Guilty of Murder</u> (2 ed., 1687), pp. 13-

↑22 Humanity   Willard, <u>Morality Not to be Relied on for Life</u> (1700), p. 9.

↑16 creature   <u>Ibid.</u>, p. 11; cf. <u>The Truly Blessed Man</u> (1700), pp. 3-

↑ 3 function   Willard, <u>Morality Not to be Relied on</u>, pp. 9-12.

p. 188

↓17 it   Cotton Mather, <u>The Everlasting Gospel</u> (1700), pp. 17-1

↓21 learning   Peter Bulkeley, <u>The Gospel-Covenant</u> (London, 1651), pp. 107-108.

↑ 7* arts   William Ames, <u>Philosophemata</u> (Leyden, 1643), pp. 20, 31-32, 73, 84, 147.

p. 189

↓ 9 <u>Nature</u>   Ames, <u>The Marrow of Sacred Divinity</u> (London, 1643), p.

↓13 Creation   James Fitch, <u>The first Principles of the Doctrine of Christ</u> (1679), p. 1.

↓15* words   Willard, <u>Heavenly Merchandize</u>, p. 9.

↑11* Logic   Ames, <u>Philosophemata</u>, p. 21.

↑ 8 Divinity   Ames, <u>Marrow</u>, p. 1.

p. 190

↓ 1 <u>Eupraxy</u>   Willard, <u>Brief Directions to a Young Scholar Designing the Ministry, for the Study of Divinity</u> (1735), pp. 3-

p. 190 continued

↓14 actions   John Wollebius, The Abridgment of Christian Divinity
                    (tr. Alexander Ross, 3 ed., London, 1660), pp. 2-3.

p. 191

↑18 Law   Richard Baxter, Reasons of the Christian Religion,
                    p. 70.

↑ 8* nature   Ames, Philosophemata, pp. 57, 21-23.

p. 192

↓11* experience   Ames, Philosophemata, p. 145.

↓13* so   Ibid., p. 66.

↓14 natural   Quaestiones, 1688; 1690; 1679; 1684.

↓15 exist   Quaestiones, 1703.

↓21 fall   Samuel Johnson (ed. Herbert and Carol Schneider, New
                    York, 1929), II, 58.

↑18 sense   Theses technologicae, No. 11, 1719.

↑ 4 plainly   Ames, Conscience with the Power and Cases Thereof
                    (London, 1643), bk. II, p. 2.

p. 193

↑ 4 senses   Ibid., bk. I, pp. 3-14, 32-33.

p. 195

↓ 1 Reason   Increase Mather, The Mystery of Christ (1686), p. 46.

↓ 5* textbooks   Johannes Maccovius, Distinctiones et regulae (Oxford,
                    1636), p. 21.

↓14* truth   Nicholaus Vedelius, Rationale Theologicum (Geneva,
                    1628), pp. 140ff.

p. 195 continued

↓16* himself   Richard Baxter et al., The Judgment of Non-Conformists
                      of the interest of Reason in matters of Religion
                      (London, 1676), p. 10.

↓18 excavated   Theses technologicae, No. 4, 1678.

↓20 theological   Quaestiones, No. VIII, 1678.

↑ 7 lights   Fitch, First Principles, p. 4.

p. 196

↓11*(2) arts   Morison, Harvard College in the Seventeenth Century,
                      pp. 260ff.; Ames, Philosophemata, pp. 121-142.

↓15* men   Ames, Philosophemata, pp. 108-109.

↑15 Nature   Ames, Conscience, bk. V, p. 100; cf. pp. 100-106.

↑ 9 theology   Theses technologicae, No. 12, 1687.

↑ 8 does   Theses ethicae, No. 1, 1670.

↑ 4 Paganism   VII Collections of the Massachusetts Historical
                      Society, viii, 357.

p. 197

↓ 4* society   Johannes Magirus, Corona Virtutum Moralium (Frankfort,
                      1601), p. 1.

↓12 tenth   Cotton, A Practical Commentary . . . upon The First
                      Epistle Generall of John, p. 234.

↓15 such   Cotton, The Way of the Churches of Christ in New-
                      England (London, 1645), pp. 92-93.

↓21* authorities   Thomas Cobbett, A Just Vindication of the Covenant
                      and Church-Estate of Children of Church-Members
                      (London, 1648), p. 213.

p. 198

↓15 pencill   Ames, Conscience, bk. V, pp. 105-108.

p. 198 continued

↑17 out   Thomas Shepard, Works (ed. John A. Albro, Boston,
                            1853), III, 28.

↑ 4 it   Ibid., III, 31.

p. 199

↓ 1 also   Shepard, Works, III, 34.

↑ 8 another   Ibid., III, 175-179.

p. 200

↓ 5 Holland   Jeremiah Dummer, A Discourse on the Holiness of the
                            Sabbath-Day (1704), p. 25.

↑19 away   Preston, The New Creature (London, 1633), p. 62.

↑12 Sterne   Ibid., p. 129.

↑ 6 naturall   Ibid., pp. 95-96.

p. 201

↓ 3 unto   Preston, Life Eternall, pt. I, p. 21.

↓22 help   Ibid., pp. 46-48.

↑19* reason   Preston, The Cuppe of Blessing (London, 1633), p. 13.

↑17 reason   Preston, Life Eternall, pt. II, p. 22.

↑ 8* judge   Preston, Cuppe of Blessing, p. 10.

↑ 4* another   Ibid., pp. 12-13.

p. 202

↓ 4 there   Hooker, The Soules Exaltation (London, 1638), p. 29.

↓ 6 heard   Hooker, Application of Redemption, p. 556.

↓ 8 creatures   Shepard, Works, III, 96-97.

p. 202 continued

↓12* grounds   Davenport, <u>The Saints Anchor-Hold</u> (London,
         1661), p. 49.

↓15 legible   Solomon Stoddard, <u>The Danger of Speedy Degeneracy</u>
         (1705), p. 11.

↑16* acquiess   John Owen, <u>Animadversions on a Treatise Intituled</u>
         <u>Fiat Lux</u> (London, 1662), p. 218.

↑13* also   <u>Ibid</u>., pp. 196-197.

p. 203

↓ 3 founded   Preston, <u>Life Eternall</u>, pt. I, pp. 53-55.

↓ 6 miracles   Samuel Lee, <u>The Joy of Faith</u> (1687), pp. 1-31.

↑ 7 it   Urian Oakes, <u>New-England Pleaded with</u> (Cambridge,
         1673), pp. 11-12.

p. 204

↓ 7 Scripture   Cotton, <u>The Grounds and Ends of the Baptisme of the</u>
         <u>Children of the Faithfull</u> (London, 1647), p. 4.

↓ 9 madnesse   Cotton, <u>A Brief Exposition Of the whole Book of</u>
         <u>Canticles</u> (London, 1642), p. 11.

↓11* command   George Phillips, <u>A Reply to a Confutation of some</u>
         <u>grounds for Infants Baptisme</u> (London, 1645),
         p. B4 recto.

↓15 Sermon by   Cotton, <u>Christ the Fountaine of Life</u> (London, 1651),
         p. 200.

↑21 Assertions   Lee, <u>Joy of Faith</u>, pp. 209-210.

↑12 believe   Willard, <u>A Brief Reply to Mr. George Kieth</u> (1703),
         p. 18.

↑ 8 it   Willard, <u>Compleat Body</u>, p. 32.

↓ 4 dignityes   John Pocklington, <u>Altare Christianum</u> (London, 1637), pp. 148-149

↑14 express   Willard, <u>Compleat Body</u>, p. 44.

↓14 inferences   <u>Ibid</u>., p. 29.

Chapter VIII: Nature

p. 207

↑ 5* God   Johann Heinrich Alsted, Physica Harmonica (1616), p. 65.

↑ 2   intent   Samuel Willard, A Compleat Body of Divinity (1726), pp. 2, 130.

p. 208

↓11* all   Samuel Lee, The Great Day of Judgment (1692), pp. 3-4.

↑20   him   Willard, Compleat Body, p. 34.

↑15* hand   John Davenport, The Saints Anchor-Hold (London, 1661), p. 173.

↑ 7* be   Thomas Hooker, An Exposition of the Principles of Religion (London, 1645), p. 2.

p. 209

↓ 5* practical   Alsted, Encyclopaedia (1649), III, 327.

↑16   it   John Preston, The Saints Qualification (London, 1633), p. 222.

↑14   language   Ibid., p. 130.

↑11   things   Preston, Life Eternall (London, 1634), pt. I, p. 5.

↑ 8   reade   Preston, Saints Qualification, p. 182.

p. 210

↓ 3   God   Preston, Life Eternall, pt. I, p. 5.

↓12   duty   William Ames, The Marrow of Sacred Divinity (London, 1643), p. 219.

↑18   commonwealth   Thomas Shepard, Works (ed. John A. Albro, Boston, 1853), I, 10; cf. II, 222.

↑14   use   Jonathan Mitchell, A Discourse of the Glory To which God hath called Believers by Jesus Christ (London, 1677), pp. 120-121.

p. 211

↓ 1 obliterated   Willard, Compleat Body, pp. 591-592 (sigs. *Gggl
                        recto - *Gggl verso).

↓10 things   Increase Mather, Soul-Saving Gospel Truths (2 ed.,
                        1712), pp. 119-120.

↑15 sort   John Cotton, A Briefe Exposition with Practicall
                        Observations upon The Whole Book of Ecclesiastes
                        (London, 1654), p. 26; cf. pp. 13, 153.

p. 212

↓19 nature   Cotton, Gods Mercie mixed with his Iustice (London,
                        1641), pp. 113-134.

↑20 Artificer   Cotton, A Briefe Exposition . . .of Ecclesiastes,
                        p. 23.

↑18 can   Ibid., p. 59.

p. 213

↓ 3* piety   Girolamo Zanchius, De Operibus Dei (1597), p. 4.

↓15 Creature   Willard, The Child's Portion (1684), pp. 77-78.

↑12 creator   Samuel Eliot Morison, Harvard College in the
                        Seventeenth Century (Cambridge, 1936), p. 131.

↑ 4 them   Cotton Mather, Christianus per Ignem (1702), pp. 10-14.

p. 214

↑21 themselves   Samuel Mather, A Testimony from the Scripture
                        against Idolatry & Superstition (Cambridge, 1670),
                        p. 9.

↑ 6 Notion   John Dunton, Letters written from New-England (The
                        Prince Society, Boston, 1867), pp. 275-276.

p. 215

↓12 dissolved   Preston, The New Creature (London, 1633), p. 52.

p. 215 continued

↓14 things   Hooker, <u>The Application of Redemption</u> (London, 1659),
                     p. 59.

↓18 al   Cotton, <u>A Brief Exposition With Practical Observations
                     Upon the whole Book of Canticles</u> (London, 1655), p. 92.

↑22* foot   Augustine, <u>Confessions</u>, IV, 20.

↑ 4 approbation   Preston, <u>Saints Qualification</u>, p. 152.

p. 216

↓ 7 repenting   <u>Ibid</u>., p. 225.

↓13 them   Hooker, <u>The Saints Guide</u> (London, 1645), p. 93.

↓17 Providence   Willard, <u>Compleat Body</u>, p. 577.

p. 218

↓ 2* utility   Ames, <u>Philosophemata</u> (Leyden, 1643), pp. 14, 21-23.

↓ 6* nature   Zanchius, <u>De Operibus Dei</u>, p. 290.

↓16 beasts   Preston, <u>Life Eternall</u>, pt. I, pp. 9-10.

↓19 form   James Fitch, <u>The first Principles of the Doctrine of
                     Christ</u> (1679), p. 18.

↓22 fell   Cotton, <u>A Briefe Exposition . . . of Ecclesiastes</u>,
                     p. 14.

↑ 5 itselfe   Hooker, <u>The Soules Exaltation</u> (London, 1638), pp. 33-34.

p. 220

↑19 atheistical   John Webster, <u>Academiarum Examen</u> (London, 1654), pp. 18-
                     20, 33-34.

↑ 4 dangers   John Hall, <u>An Humble Motion to The Parliament of
                     England Concerning The Advancement of Learning</u> (London,
                     1649), pp. 41, 44; cf. Seth Ward, <u>Vindiciae Academiarum</u>
                     (Oxford, 1654), pp. 1-2.

p. 221

↓ 2 follow   Morison, The Founding of Harvard College (Cambridge, 1935), p. 77.

↓15 System   Samuel Sewall, Diary, V Collections of the Massachu-setts Historical Society, vii, 31.

↓22* warily   Charles Morton, MS. Compendium Physicae (copied by Jeremiah Gridley; Massachusetts Historical Society), Preface.

↑18* Boyle   Ibid., p. 4.

↑11 vary   Morton, The Spirit of Man (1693), p. 27.

↑ 4 Principles   Increase Mather, ΚΟΜΗΤΟΓΡΑΦΙΑ; or A Discourse Concerning Comets (1683), pp. 3, 7.

p. 222

↓ 2 Question   Cotton Mather, Eleutheria (London, 1698), p. 78.

p. 223

↓17 Wisdom   Samuel Lee, The Joy of Faith (1687), pp. 212-214, 218; cf. p. 209.

↑ 8 discover   Increase Mather, ΚΟΜΗΤΟΓΡΑΦΙΑ, p. A3 verso.

p. 224

↓ 6* God   Davenport, Saints Anchor-Hold, p. 155.

↓12 it   Willard, Compleat Body, pp. 133ff.

↑21* natures   Zanchius, De Operibus Dei, pp. 1062-1081; cf. John Wollebius, The Abridgment of Christian Divinity (tr. Alexander Ross, 3 ed., London, 1660), pp. 35ff.

↑16* fortuitously Urian Oakes, The Soveraign Efficacy of Divine Providence (1682), pp. 2-3.

↑10 indigence   Wollebius, Abridgment, p. 57.

p. 224 continued

↑ 1* Spinoza   Petro van Mastricht, <u>Theoretico-Practica Theologia</u>
                      (1699), pp. 396-397.

p. 225

↓17 God   Ames, <u>Marrow</u>, pp. 42-43.

↑ 4 thing   Preston, <u>The New Covenant</u> (London, 1629), pp. 159-16

p. 226

↓ 8 this   Willard, <u>Compleat Body</u>, p. 38.

↓10 Master-piece   Jonathan Mitchell, <u>Discourse of the Glory</u>, p. 64.

↓16 lives   Fitch, <u>First Principles</u>, pp. 19-20.

↓20 whole   William Hubbard, <u>The Happiness of a People in the
                      Wisdome of their Rulers Directing</u> (1676), p. 16.

↑18 wisdome   Fitch, <u>First Principles</u>, p. 13.

↑16 things   Ames, <u>Marrow</u>, pp. 40-41.

↑15 nature   Preston, <u>New Covenant</u>, p. 46.

↑10 returne   Preston, <u>New Creature</u>, p. 97.

↑ 7 bodies   Cotton, <u>A Briefe Exposition . . . of Ecclesiastes</u>,
                      p. 66.

↑ 3 Perpetuity   Willard, <u>Compleat Body</u>, p. 137; cf. pp. 70, 135.

p. 227

↓19 eyes   Davenport, <u>The Knowledge of Christ Indispensably
                      required of all men that would be saved</u> (London,
                      1653), pp. 64ff.

↑13 <u>multiplicanda</u> Cotton, <u>The Way of Congregational Churches Cleared</u>
                      (London, 1648), pt. I, p. 42.

↑11 miracles   Samuel Nowell, <u>Abraham in Arms</u> (1678), p. 11.

p. 227 continued

↑ 2 another   Hooker, <u>Soules Exaltation</u>, p. 106.

p. 228

↓12* nature   William Perkins, <u>Works</u>, I (London, 1626), p. 156.

↑ 9 eccentricities Preston, <u>Life Eternall</u>, pt. I, p. 33.

p. 229

↑ 9 providence   John Winthrop, <u>Winthrop's Journal</u>, "<u>History of New</u>
                     <u>England</u>," 1630-1649 (ed. J. K. Hosmer, New York,
                     1908), II, 18; 354-355; 321-322; 126.

p. 230

↓ 5 way   Preston, <u>Sinnes Overthrow</u> (London, 1635), p. 241.

↓16 immediately   Fitch, <u>First Principles</u>, p. 13; cf. p. 22.

p. 231

↓17 thereof   Increase Mather, <u>An Essay for the Recording of</u>
                     <u>Illustrious Providences</u> [1684] (ed. George Offor,
                     as <u>Remarkable Providences</u>, London, 1856), p. 70

↓21 lightning   <u>Ibid</u>., p. 91.

↑21 disacknowl-   <u>Ibid</u>., p. 92.
     edged

↑17 year   Increase Mather, ΚΟΜΗΤΟΓΡΑΦΙΑ, pp. 18, 21.

↑14* it   Increase Mather, <u>A Discourse Concerning Earthquakes</u>
                     (1706), pp. 5-8.

↑ 9 pass   Increase Mather, <u>The Voice of God in Stormy Winds</u>
                     (1704), pp. 16-17, 42.

p. 232

↓10* order   Perkins, <u>Works</u>, I, 15.

p. 232 continued

↓20 responsible   James Allen, Joshua Moody, et al., <u>The Principles</u>
                     <u>of the Protestant Religion Maintained</u> (1690), pp. 70-
                     71.

↑12* understood   Alsted, <u>Physica Harmonica</u>, pp. 61-63.

↑ 9 counsel   Fitch, <u>First Principles</u>, p. 15.

↑ 1 them   Willard, <u>Compleat Body</u>, p. 137.

p. 233

↑18 reason   Willard, <u>A Brief Reply to Mr. George Kieth</u> (1703),
                     <u>passim</u>.

↑ 6 Creature   <u>Ibid</u>., p. 26.

↑ 4 shortned   Preston, <u>The Breast-Plate of Faith and Love</u> (London,
                     1634), pt. II, pp. 164-166.

p. 234

↓ 3 corrupted   Ames, <u>Marrow</u>, pp. 27-28.

↓ 7* stands   Richard Sibbes, <u>Works</u> (ed. Alexander R. Grosart,
                     Edinburgh, 1862-64), I, 204-205.

↓12 Causes   Willard, <u>Compleat Body</u>, p. 143.

↑21 meanes   Preston, <u>Life Eternall</u>, pt. II, p. 150.

↑19 Means   Willard, <u>Compleat Body</u>, p. 91.

p. 235

↓ 4 perceiveable   Ames, <u>Marrow</u>, pp. 39-40.

↑21 appointment   Oakes, <u>Soveraign Efficacy</u>, pp. 6-8.

Chapter IX: The Nature of Man

p. 242

↓ 4   receiued   F. N. Coeffeteau, <u>A Table of Humane Passions</u> (London,
                      1621), pp. a5 verso - a7 recto.

↑20   refused   Samuel Willard, <u>A Compleat Body of Divinity</u> (1726),
                      pp. 119-120, 512.

p. 243

↑22* God   Pierre de la Primaudaye, <u>The French Academie</u> (London,
                      1602-05), pt. I, pp. 39, 14-16.

↑18   faculties   John Ball, <u>A Treatise of Faith</u> (London, 1632), pp. 138-
                      139; cf. William Pemble, "Vindiciae Gratiae," in
                      <u>Workes</u> (Oxford, 1659), pp. 111-114.

p. 244

↓ 1* nature   <u>French Academie</u>, pt. II, p. 142.

↓ 7* poynt   Thomas Hooker, "Preparing for Christ," Appendix to
                      <u>The Unbeleevers Preparing for Christ</u> (London, 1638),
                      p. 26.

↓ 9   confused   Willard, <u>Compleat Body</u>, p. 454.

↓11   men   <u>Ibid</u>., p. 26.

p. 245

↓ 9*(1) nature   George Sidney Brett, <u>A History of Psychology</u> (London,
                      1912-21), II, 156, 163; and H. M. Gardiner, Ruth Clark
                      Metcalf, John G. Beebe-Center, <u>Feeling and Emotion; a</u>
                      <u>history of theories</u> (New York, 1937), pp. 121-123.

p. 246

↓13   known   Willard, <u>Compleat Body</u>, p. 41.

↓17* Truth   Willard, <u>Heavenly Merchandize</u> (1686), pp. 5-6.

↓20   body   Increase Mather, <u>An Essay for the Recording of Illus-</u>
                      <u>trious Providences</u> [1684] (ed. George Offor, as
                      <u>Remarkable Providences</u>, London, 1856), p. 83.

p. 246 continued

↓21 body   Mock theses physicae, No. 15; cf. Timothy Bright,
                         A Treatise of Melancholy [1 ed., 1586] (London, 1616)
                         pp. 42-46.

↑18 work   Willard, Compleat Body, p. 123; cf. Brett, A History
                         of Psychology, II, 72; Johannes Magirus, Physiologiae
                         Peripateticae (Geneva, 1638), pp. 570-572; French
                         Academie, pt. II, pp. 146-155.

↑ 1* bread   Girolamo Zanchius, De Operibus Dei Intra Spacium
                         Sex Dierum Creatis Opus (1597), p. 736.

p. 247

↓ 3* goals   Edward Reynolds, A Treatise of the Passions and
                         Faculties of the Soule of Man (London, 1658),
                         pp. 18-20.

↓10* Reason   Ibid., p. 24.

↑22 Souls   Cotton Mather, The Serviceable Man (1690), p. 10.

↑19 them   John Huarte, Examen de Ingenios (London, 1596), p. 61

↑11* soul   Reynolds, Treatise of the Passions, p. 403.

↑ 5* phansie   John Preston, An Elegant and Lively Description of
                         Spirituall Life and Death (London, 1636), p. 87.

p. 248

↓13 Divinity   Willard, Compleat Body, pp. 123-124.

↓22* things   French Academie, pt. II, p. 145.

↑14 Imagination   Coeffeteau, Table of Humane Passions, p. a4 recto.

↑ 5 done   William Ames, Conscience with the Power and Cases
                         Thereof (London, 1643), bk. I, p. 15; cf. The Marrow
                         of Sacred Divinity (London, 1643), p. 5.

↑ 2* much   Hooker, The Unbeleevers Preparing for Christ, p. 32.

p. 249

↓ 1 Understanding   Willard, The Christians Exercise by Satans Tempta-
                     tions (1701), p. 17.

↓ 5 understanding   Ibid., pp. 219-220; Compleat Body, p. 191.

↓ 8 intellect   Theses physicae, No. 16, 1647; No. 14, 1653 (Aug.
                     10); No. 16, 1678.

↓11 mind   Quaestiones, No. 2, 1686.

↓12 it   Quaestio, 1658.

↑ 9 judgement   Ames, Conscience, bk. I, p. 16.

↑ 6 with   Preston, Sinnes Overthrow (London, 1635), p. 49.

↑ 4 acts   Preston, The Position of John Preston (London, 1654),
                     p. 13.

p. 250

↓ 4 body   John Cotton, The way of Life (London, 1641), pp. 200-
                     201; Gods Mercie mixed with his Iustice (London, 1641),
                     pp. 3-4.

↑22 all   Cotton, Way of Life, pp. 205-206.

↑18 Mover   Willard, Compleat Body, p. 103.

↑10* pursue   French Academie, pt. II, pp. 205-207; Reynolds,
                     Treatise of the Passions, pp. 517-518.

↑ 8 intellect   Theses physicae, No. 14, 1653 (Aug. 9).

↑ 6* insoluble   Otho Casmannus, Psychologia Anthropologica (Hanover,
                     1594), pp. 138-140.

p. 251

↓ 3 affections   Preston, The Breast-Plate of Faith and Love (London,
     will follow   1634), pt. II, p. 90.

↓10* the will   Hooker, The Unbeleevers Preparing for Christ, p. 56.

p. 251 continued

↓18   them   Hooker, The Soules Preparation for Christ (London, 1638), p. 30.

↑21* condition   John Davenport, The Saints Anchor-Hold (London, 1661), pp. 65-67.

↑16   obstinacie   Hooker, The Christians Two Chiefe Lessons (London, 164(p. 10.

↑ 1* destructive   Reynolds, Treatise of the Passions, pp. 31-32.

p. 252

↓ 8* physically   French Academie, pt. II, p. 230.

↓15   it   Preston, Sinnes Overthrow, p. 187.

↑20* motions   French Academie, pt. II, pp. 200-203.

↑14* higher   Reynolds, Treatise of the Passions, p. 43.

↑ 6* Ministers   Ibid., p. 44.

p. 253

↓ 2   Understanding   Willard, The Truly Blessed Man (1700), p. 470; cf. Compleat Body, p. 455.

↓12   Affections   Urian Oakes, New-England Pleaded with (Cambridge, 1673), p. 11.

↑15   soule   Hooker, The Soules Vocation (London, 1638), pp. 152-153.

p. 254

↓ 1   formally   Theses physicae, No. 16, 1653 (Aug. 10); cf. French Academie, pt. II, pp. 229-249.

↓11   misery   Gardiner et al., Feeling and Emotion, p. 31.

↓12   Nature   Preston, The New Creature (London, 1633), p. 110.

p. 254 continued

↓14 Humanity   Willard, <u>Spiritual Desertions Discovered and Remedied</u> (1699), pp. 69-70.

↓18 them   Willard, <u>Mercy Magnified on a penitent Prodigal</u> (1684), p. 67.

↑13* service   Reynolds, <u>Treatise of the Passions</u>, p. 60.

↑ 6* will   Willard, <u>Christians Exercise</u>, p. 166.

p. 255

↓ 3 for   Willard, <u>The Mourners Cordial</u> (1691), pp. 35-36.

↓19 <u>Commandments</u>   <u>Ibid</u>., pp. 37-38.

p. 256

↑12 Confusion   Willard, <u>Compleat Body</u>, p. 127.

p. 257

↓ 3 ought   Coeffeteau, <u>Table of Humane Passions</u>, p. a7 recto.

↓ 5 obeyeth   Sir William Cornwallyes, <u>Essayes</u> (London, 1610), Essay 36.

↓13 cunning   J. F. Senault, <u>The Use of Passions</u> (London, 1649), pp. 102-103; cf. Philippe de Mornay, <u>The True Knowledge of a Mans Owne Selfe</u> (London, 1602), pp. 191-192; <u>French Academie</u>, pt. II, pp. 191, 218, 236.

↑ 9 passions   Thomas Wright, <u>The Passions of the minde in generall</u> (London, 1604), pp. 51-52; Senault, <u>Use of Passions</u>, p. 19.

↑ 6* experience Reynolds, <u>Treatise of the Passions</u>, p. 27.

↑ 2 us   Willard, <u>Christians Exercise</u>, p. 94.

p. 258

↓16* indeed   Richard Sibbes, <u>Works</u> (ed. Alexander R. Grosart,
                   Edinburgh, 1862-64), I, 178-191.

↓22 indeed   Willard, <u>Ne Sutor ultra Crepidam</u> (1681), p. 2.

↑ 1 it   Hooker, <u>The Application of Redemption</u> (London, 1659),
                   p. 161.

p. 259

↓ 5 good   <u>Ibid</u>., p. 166.

↓ 8* senses   Willard, <u>Christians Exercise</u>, pp. 162-163.

↓12 comming   Hooker, <u>The Soules Ingrafting into Christ</u>, (London,
                   1637), p. 18.

↓16 understanding Senault, <u>Use of Passions</u>, pp. 74-75.

↓22 soule   Preston, <u>Sinnes Overthrow</u>, p. 16.

↑17 them   Preston, <u>The Saints Qualification</u> (London, 1633),
                   p. 49.

p. 260

↓ 3* undoing   Willard, <u>Heavenly Merchandize</u>, pp. 94-96.

↓12* perverse   William Allen, <u>A Discourse of the Nature, Ends,</u>
                   <u>and Difference of the Two Covenants</u> (London, 1673),
                   pp. 170ff.

↓17* will   Brett, <u>A History of Psychology</u>, II, 128-130.

↑ 5 understanding Ames, <u>Conscience</u>, bk. I, p. 16.

↑ 2* independently Cf. William Strong, <u>A Treatise Shewing the Subordin-</u>
                   <u>ation of the Will of Man</u> (London, 1657), p. 28;
                   Willard, <u>Reformation The Great Duty of an Afflicted</u>
                   <u>People</u> (1694), p. 29; Allen, <u>A Discourse of the</u>
                   <u>. . . Two Covenants</u>, pp. 178, 180-181; Hooker,
                   <u>The Unbeleevers Preparing for Christ</u>, pp. 127-128.

p. 261

↓ 3* Understanding   Reynolds, Treatise of the Passions, p. 542.

↓12   exceedingly   Preston, Sinnes Overthrow, p. 209.

↓15   under   Ibid., pp. 219, 196.

↑21* bounds   Eliphalet Adams, A Discourse Putting Christians In Mind To be Ready to Every Good Work (1706), p. 22.

↑ 2* Sense   Reynolds, Treatise of the Passions, p. 44.

↑ 1* thereof   Ibid., p. 495.

p. 262

↑20   things   Cornwallyes, Essayes, pp. N5 recto - N5 verso; cf. Wright, Passions of the minde, pp. 8-11; cf. also French Academie, pt. I, pp. 27-31.

↑11   reason   Wright, Passions of the minde, pp. 53-59; Senault, Use of Passions, p. 17.

↑ 5* Nature   Reynolds, Treatise of the Passions, p. 65.

p. 263

↓ 7   purpose   Preston, Saints Qualification, p. 59.

↓ 9   discourse   Willard, Christians Exercise, pp. 220-221; Cotton Mather, Seven Select Lectures (London, 1695), pp. 149-152.

↓13* agree   Cf. Pemble, Workes, p. 75.

p. 264

↓ 7* Humane   Reynolds, Treatise of the Passions, p. 62.

↓19   effect   Zanchius, The Whole Body of Christian Religion (tr. D. Ralph Winterton, London, 1659), pp. 53-61.

↑18   forced   Willard, Compleat Body, p. 455; cf. Reynolds, Treatise of the Passions, pp. 539-540.

p. 264 continued

↑ 7* him   Zacharias Ursinus, <u>The Summe of Christian Religion</u> (tr. Henry Passy, London, 1633), pp. 213-214.

↑ 3   reason   Cotton, <u>A Practical Commentary . . . upon The First Epistle Generall of John</u> (London, 1656), pp. 247-248.

p. 265

↓ 3   free   Preston, <u>Mount Ebal</u> (London, 1638), p. 4; cf. Ames, <u>Conscience</u>, bk. III, pp. 91-92.

↓ 5   Obedience   John Rogers, <u>A Sermon Preached before His Excellency the Governour</u> (1706), p. 16.

↓10   grounds   Willard, <u>Mercy Magnified</u>, p. 176.

↑15* Soul   Reynolds, <u>Treatise of the Passions</u>, pp. 444-445.

↑ 1* memory   Ames, <u>Philosophemata</u> (Leyden, 1643), p. 170.

p. 266

↓ 5   disposition Alexander Richardson, <u>The Logicians School-Master</u> (London, 1657), p. 247.

↓17* faculty   Rudolph Snell, <u>Partitiones Physicae</u> (1594), pp. 218-219.

↑19 <u>all</u>   In Cotton Mather, <u>Christianus per Ignem</u> (1702), p. 2.

p. 267

↑14* corporeality <u>French Academie</u>, pt. II, p. 151.

p. 268

↓ 4   Mathematicks Wright, <u>Passions of the minde</u>, pp. 300-306.

↑ 3* Image   Reynolds, <u>Treatise of the Passions</u>, pp. 445-446.

p. 269

↓15* Stierius   Joannes Stierius, <u>Praecepta Doctrinae</u> (London, 1671), "Praecepta Physicae," p. 61.

↓19 perfection   Richard Hooker, <u>Of the Laws of Ecclesiastical Polity,</u> I, vi, 1.

p. 270

↓16 parents   Zanchius, <u>Whole Body of Christian Religion</u>, p. 68.

↓17 it   Preston, <u>Saints Qualification</u>, p. 181-182.

↑16* <u>sensu</u>   Zanchius, <u>De Operibus Dei</u>, pp. 799ff.

↑ 6* Dominion   Reynolds, <u>Treatise of the Passions</u>, pp. 457-458.

p. 271

↓ 5 all   Preston, <u>Life Eternall</u> (London, 1634), pp. 17-18.

p. 272

↑14* do   Ames, <u>Philosophemata</u>, p. 66.

↑ 8* to time   Alsted, <u>Encyclopaedia</u> (1649), I, 74.

p. 273

↑19 things   Edward, Lord Herbert of Cherbury, <u>De Veritate</u> (tr. with an introduction by Meyrick H. Carré, University of Bristol, Eng., 1937), p. 111.

↑ 3 being   <u>Ibid</u>., p. 233.

p. 274

↓ 3 objects   <u>Ibid</u>., p. 80; cf. pp. 129ff.

↓ 5 object   Cotton, <u>A Briefe Exposition with Practicall Observations upon The Whole Book of Ecclesiastes</u> (London, 1654), p. 266.

↓17 universe   Lord Herbert of Cherbury, <u>De Veritate</u>, pp. 108ff.

p. 274 continued

↓22 them   Ibid., p. 106.

↑17 whole   Ibid., p. 111.

p. 275

↓11* souls   French Academie, pt. II, pp. 153-154, 171, 219, 244.

↑ 2 ill   Lord Herbert of Cherbury, De Veritate, p. 86.

p. 276

↓ 5 all   Ibid., p. 132.

↓15 sensation   Ibid., pp. 122ff.

↑ 1 faith   Ibid., p. 76.

p. 277

↓ 7* arguments   Alsted, Encyclopaedia, I, 51.

↓ 9 nature   Lord Herbert of Cherbury, De Veritate, pp. 289-307.

↓18 himselfe   Ames, Marrow, p. 62.

↓20 intellect   Theses physicae, No. 12, 1646.

↑ 9 Will   Willard, Compleat Body, pp. 573-574.

Chapter X: The Means of Conversion

p.   281

↓13   things   John Preston, <u>Sinnes Overthrow</u> (London, 1635),
                      p. 56.   (Incorrect).

↓20   instantaneous   Samuel Willard, <u>A Compleat Body of Divinity</u> (1726),
                      p. 441.

↑14   are   Preston, <u>Sinnes Overthrow</u>, p. 202.

↑ 4   minde   <u>Ibid.</u>, p. 56.

p.   282

↓ 6   evill   Preston, The Position of John Preston (London,
                      1654), p. 12.

↓10   it   Preston, <u>The Breast-Plate of Faith and Love</u>
                      (London, 1634), pt. I, p. 15.

↑15* affection   John Davenport, <u>The Saints Anchor-Hold</u> (London,
                      1661), pp. 67-69.

↑ 8* goodnesse   <u>Ibid.</u>, p. 64.

p.   283

↓ 2* answereth   <u>Ibid.</u>, p. 237.

↓ 8   Justice   J. F. Senault, <u>The Use of Passions</u> (London, 1649),
                      p. 61; cf. p. 65:   man "must become pious if he
                      will be reasonable."

↓16* ignorant   Pierre de la Primaudaye, <u>The French Academie</u>
                      (London, 1602-05), pt. II, p. 188.

↓19   manner   Preston, <u>Sinnes Overthrow</u>, p. 50.

↑ 8* devell-ward   Thomas Hooker, "Preparing for Christ," pp. 20-26,
                      in <u>The Unbeleevers Preparing for Christ</u> (London,
                      1638).

↑ 1   them   Willard, <u>Compleat Body</u>, p. 493.

p. 284

↓ 7* frame   Hooker, The Covenant of Grace Opened (London,
                    1649), p. 31; cf. especially Willard, Compleat
                    Body, p. 802.

↑20 uses   Willard, Compleat Body, p. 450.

↑11 above   Ibid., pp. 494-495.

↑ 9 remembred   Hooker, The·Saints Dignitie, and Dutie
                    (London, 1651), p. 125.

p. 285

↓15 sufficient   William Ames, Conscience with the Power and
                    Cases Thereof (London, 1643), bk. I, p. 17.

↑15 him   Hooker, The Soules Vocation (London, 1638),
                    pp. 288-289.

p. 286

↓ 3* together   Increase Mather, Two Plain and Practical Discourses
                    Concerning Hardness of Heart (London, 1699), p. 94.

↑20 Subjectively   Willard, Compleat Body, p. 815.

↑12 purpose   Hooker, Soules Vocation, p. 64.

↑ 7 Considerations Jonathan Mitchell, A Discourse of the Glory To
                    which God hath called Believers by Jesus Christ
                    (London, 1677), p. 164.

p. 288

↓ 3 body   Girolamo Zanchius, The Whole Body of Christian
                    Religion (tr. D. Ralph Winterton, London, 1659),
                    pp. 238-239.

↓19 another   William Stoughton, New-Englands True Interest;
                    Not to Lie (Cambridge, 1670), p. 12.

↓20 doing   Willard, Compleat Body, p. 443.

p. 288 continued

↓22 it   Willard, <u>Mercy Magnified on a penitent Prodigal</u>
                       (1684), p. 154.

↓22 nature   Willard, <u>Spiritual Desertions Discovered and
                       Remedied</u> (1699), p. 71.

↑14 actions   Willard, <u>Compleat Body</u>, p. 451.

p. 289

↑ 6 them   Ames, <u>The Marrow of Sacred Divinity</u> (London, 1643),
                       p. 143.

↑ 4 means   Hooker, <u>The Application of Redemption</u> (London, 1659),
                       p. 343.

↑ 2 life   Hooker, <u>The Soules Humiliation</u> (London, 1638), pp. 59-60.

p. 290

↓12 Soul   Increase Mather, <u>Ichabod</u> (1702), pp. 28-29; cf. Richard
                       Mather, <u>Church-Government and Church-Covenant Discussed</u>
                       (London, 1643), p. 79.

↓14 Word   John Cotton, <u>The way of Life</u> (London, 1641), p. 12.

↑19 not   Hooker, <u>Soules Vocation</u>, pp. 62-63.

↑14 confirme   Hooker, <u>The Soules Preparation for Christ</u> (London,
                       1638), p. 138.

↑ 4 sermons   Joseph Belcher, "God Giveth the Increase," [1722],
                       in E. Burgess, <u>The Dedham Pulpit</u> (Boston, 1840),
                       p. 198; cf. Willard, <u>The Best Priviledge</u> (1701),
                       p. 16.

p. 291

↓ 3* prescribes   Richard Sibbes, <u>Works</u> (ed. Alexander B. Grosart,
                       Edinburgh, 1862-64), I, 225.

↓ 8 faith   Cotton, <u>Gods Mercie mixed with his Iustice</u> (London,
                       1641), p. 90.

↓10* vain   Davenport, <u>Saints Anchor-Hold</u>, p. 26.

p. 291 continued

↓12 others   Charles Chauncy, The Plain Doctrin of the Justification of a Sinner in the sight of God (London, 1659), p. 75.

↓14 it   Hooker, "The Poore Doubting Christian," in The Saints Cordials (London, 1629), p. 361.

↓19* them not   Preston, An Elegant and Lively Description of Spirituall Life and Death (London, 1636), p. 82.

↓20 them   Hooker, Soules Humiliation, p. 11.

↑18* Lord   Hooker, Heavens Treasury Opened (London, 1645), p. 115.

↑ 5 had   Richard Mather, Church-Government and Church-Covenant Discussed, p. 34.

p. 292

↓14* yeeld   Hooker, "Preparing for Christ," p. 30, in The Unbeleever Preparing for Christ.

↓20 intellect   Willard, Compleat Body, pp. 326-330.

↑21 Man   Ibid., pp. 819-820.

↑17 believe   Ibid., pp. 814-819.

↑14 Soul   Ibid., p. 807.

↑ 9 knowledge   Willard, Mercy Magnified, p. 150.

↑ 7 them   Willard, The Barren Fig Trees Doom (1691), p. 3.

↑ 3 value   Urian Oakes, New-England Pleaded with (Cambridge, 1673), p. 13.

p. 293

↓ 5 Soul   Ebenezer Pemberton, Preface to Willard, Some Brief Sacramental Meditations Preparatory for Communion at the Great Ordinance of the Supper (2 ed., 1743), p. ii.

↓11 faith   Preston, Life Eternall (London, 1634), pt. I, p. 20.

p. 293 continued

↓16* them   Sibbes, Works, I, 245.

↑19 powers   Willard, Compleat Body, p. 440.

↑11 artificials   Cotton, Christ the Fountaine of Life (London, 1651),
                         pp. 236-237.

↑ 8 Knowledge   Willard, Compleat Body, p. 437.

↑ 1 it   Hooker, Application of Redemption, pp. 86-87.

p. 294

↓ 6 Scripture   Ibid., p. 50.

↓10* other   Willard, A Brief Discourse of Justification (1686),
                         pp. 86-87.

↓18 thereto   Willard, The Truly Blessed Man (1700), pp. 445-446.

↑21 man   Hooker, Application of Redemption, p. 86.

↑11 affections   Thomas Wright, The Passions of the minde in generall
                         (London, 1604), p. 2.

↑ 5 affections   Willard, Compleat Body, p. 31.

↑ 2* delight   Sibbes, Works, I, ci.

p. 295

↓ 1 hearts   Hooker, Soules Preparation for Christ, p. 70.

↓ 9 Actions   Willard, Compleat Body, p. 812.

↓16 sinners   Joseph Belcher, "God Giveth the Increase," [1722],
                         in E. Burgess, The Dedham Pulpit, p. 200.

↑19 Jesus   Hooker, The Soules Implantation (London, 1637), p. 58.

↑ 3 conversion   Cotton, A Practical Commentary . . . upon The First
                         Epistle Generall of John (London, 1656), p. 169.

p. 296

↓15 confound thee   Hooker, <u>The Soules Exaltation</u> (London, 1638), p. 28.

↑13* repentance   William Perkins, "The Art of Prophecying," in <u>Workes</u> (London, 1626-31), II, p. 645.

↑ 7 conception   Michael Wigglesworth, "The prayse of Eloquence," in Samuel Eliot Morison, <u>Harvard College in the Seventeenth Century</u> (Cambridge, 1936), p. 180.

p. 297

↓ 9* word   Hooker, <u>The Unbeleevers Preparing for Christ</u>, p. 160.

↓14 you   Cotton, <u>Christ the Fountaine of Life</u>, pp. 173-174.

↑22 aright   Hooker, <u>Application of Redemption</u>, p. 372.

↑19 Christ   Chauncy, <u>Plain Doctrin of the Justification of a Sinner</u>, p. 75.

↑13 hell   Hooker, <u>Soules Implantation</u>, p. 77.

p. 298

↓ 1 Christ   Hooker, <u>Saints Dignitie</u>, p. 135.

↑ 9 done   Preston, <u>The New Creature</u> (London, 1633), pp. 156-157.

↑ 1 welfare   Hooker, <u>A Survey of the Summe of Church-Discipline</u> (London, 1648), p. C2 recto.

p. 299

↓ 4 effects   Cotton, <u>The Grounds and Ends of the Baptisme of the Children of the Faithfull</u> (London, 1647), p. 15.

Chapter XI: Rhetoric

p.   300

↓ 3   him   John Cotton, A Brief Exposition Of the whole Book
                     of Canticles (London, 1642), p. 168.

↑13   evidence   Thomas Hooker, The Soules Implantation (London, 1637),
                     p. 65.

↑12   meanest   Hooker, A Survey of the Summe of Church-Discipline
                     (London, 1648), pt. I, p. 112.

↑11   than fire   Thomas Shepard, Works (ed. John A. Albro, Boston,
                     1853), III, 380.

↑ 8   misery   Ibid., I, clxxxvi.

↑ 7   God   Cotton, A Briefe Exposition with Practicall Observa-
                     tions upon The Whole Book of Ecclesiastes (London,
                     1654), p. 269.

↑ 5   hands   William Ames, Conscience with the Power and Cases
                     Thereof (London, 1643), bk. IV, pp. 77-78.

p.   301

↓ 1   stir   Hooker, The Application of Redemption (London, 1659),
                     pp. 196-197.

↓ 6   stand   Hooker, The Soules Preparation for Christ (London,
                     1638), p. 63; The Soules Implantation, p. 67.

↓10   minister   Hooker, Application of Redemption, p. 195; Soules
                     Implantation, pp. 21, 61.

↓16   work   Samuel Willard, The Truly Blessed Man (1700), p. 426.

↑18   affection   Ames, Conscience, bk. IV, p. 72.

↑14   people   Hooker, Soules Implantation, p. 66.

↑11* himself   William Perkins, "The Art of Prophecying," in Workes
                     (London, 1626-31), II, 671.

↑ 5   Ministery   Cotton, A Brief Exposition Of the whole Book of
                     Canticles, p. 112.

p. 302

↓ 3   Sentences   Increase Mather, A Plain Discourse (1713), p. iv.

↓ 4   expressions   Shepard, Works, III, 278.

↓ 6   altar   The Bay Psalm Book (Cambridge, 1640), Preface.

↓ 7   milke   Cotton, A Briefe Exposition . . . of Ecclesiastes,
                      p. 269.

↓17 day   Hooker, Application of Redemption, p. 201.

↓21* him   Perkins, "Art of Prophecying," in Workes, II, 670.

↑18 Christ   Hooker, Soules Preparation for Christ, pp. 60-61.

p. 303

↓10 Rhetorick   John Webster, Academiarum Examen (London, 1654),
                      pp. 88-90.

↓20* minde   Joseph Sedgwick, Learning's Necessity to an Able
                      Minister of the Gospel (London, 1653), p. 55.

p. 305

↓20* handmaids   Perkins, "Art of Prophecying," in Workes, II, 645.

↑19 God   Cotton Mather, Optanda (1692), p. 54.

p. 306

↓ 9   will   Thomas Wilson, The Arte of Rhetorique [London, 1560]
                      (ed. G. H. Mair, Oxford, 1909), Preface.

↓14 large   Wilson, The Rule of Reason (London, 1552), p. 5
                      recto.

↓20 waie   Ibid., p. 4 recto.

↑11* One   Edward Reynolds, A Treatise of the Passions and
                      Faculties of the Soule of Man (London, 1658),
                      pp. 504-512; cf. pp. 20-21.

↑ 6   grown   Cotton Mather, Corderius Americanus (1708), p. 28.

p. 307

↓20* persuasion   Aristotle, Rhetoric, 1355[h].

p. 308

↓ 2 abused   Alexander Richardson, "Rhetorical Notes," in The Logicians School-Master (London, 1657), pp. 32, 50, 35.

↑ 8 Eupraxy   Ibid., p. 30.

p. 309

↑18 sure   Richardson, Logicians School-Master, p. 11.

p. 310

↓14* aright   William Chappell, The Use of Holy Scripture (London, 1653), p. 62; cf. Willard, A Compleat Body of Divinity (1726), pp. 31-32.

↓22* God   Charles Chauncy, Gods Mercy, Shewed to his People (Cambridge, 1655), pp. 37, 48.

↑18 Signi   James Allen, Joshua Moody et al., The Principles of the Protestant Religion Maintained (1690), p. 21.

↑ 5 perswasiuely   Richard Bernard, The Faithfull Shepherd (London, 1621), pp. 47-49; cf. pp. 44-46, 51, 175-205.

p. 311

↓16* eloquence   John Smith, The Mysterie of Rhetorick Unveil'd (London, 1673), pp. A5 recto - A6 verso.

↑12* Arts   Perkins, "Art of Prophecying," in Workes, II, 650.

↑ 4 hearers   Cotton, Gods Mercie mixed with his Iustice (London, 1641), pp. A2 verso - A3 recto.

p. 314

↓13* it   Gerhard Joannes Vossius, Rhetorices Contractae (Oxford, 1651), pp. 116ff.

p. 314 continued

↑18* Vossius   Ibid., p. 3.

↑15* pronunciare   Ibid., p. 4.

p. 315

↓ 4 figures   Wilson, Arte of Rhetorique, p. 161.

p. 316

↓14* philosophical   Henry Schorus, Specimen et forma legitime tradendi
                     sermonis (1572), p. 51.

↑17* disposition   Abraham Fraunce, The Lawiers Logike (London, 1588),
                     p. 115 recto.

p. 317

↑20 thing   Wilson, Arte of Rhetorique, p. 23.

↑15* persuading   Vossius, Rhetorices Contractae, pp. 15-16.

p. 319

↓ 7* series   Gulielmus Scribonius, Edition of Omer Talon's
                     Rhetorica (Basle, 1589), pp. 3-4 and following.

↑16* strongly   Thomas Blount, The Academie of Eloquence (London,
                     1683), p. 1; cf. Smith, Mysterie of Rhetorick
                     Unveil'd, pp. 2-4.

↑ 2* nomine   Charles Butler, Rhetoricae Libri Duo (London, 1642),
                     Preface.

p. 321

↓10* rhetoricians   Schorus, Specimen et forma, p. 50.

↓18 Logick   Richardson, Logicians School-Master, p. 55.

↑11* writings   Schorus, Specimen et forma, p. 35.

p.   321 continued

↑ 1* more   George Draudius, Bibliotheca Classica (1611),
                   pp. 1090-1094; cf. Henry Diest, De Ratione Studii
                   Theologici (2 ed., Amsterdam, 1654), pp. 73-74.

p.   324

↓20* eupraxia   Talon, Rhetorica, p. 1.

p.   325

↓ 2* powerfully   Blount, Academie of Eloquence, p. 1.

↓ 6* hand   Smith, Mysterie of Rhetorick Unveil'd, p. 1.

p.   326

↑12* rhetoric   George Downame, Commentarii in P. Rami Regii Pro-
                   fessoris Dialecticam (London, 1669), p. 8.

p.   327

↓12 oration   Theses rhetoricae, No. 1, 1687; No. 1, 1689; No. 1
                   1691.

↑ 5 meaning   Willard, Compleat Body, p. 32.

p.   328

↓ 4 it   Ibid., p. 33.

↓ 8 men   Willard, Spiritual Desertions Discovered and Remedied
                   (1699), pp. 12-13.

↓16 thereof   Samuel Mather, A Testimony from the Scripture against
                   Idolatry & Superstition (Cambridge, 1670), p. 7.

Chapter XII: The Plain Style

p. 331

↑ 5 done   Thomas Allen, Preface to John Cotton, An Exposition
                         upon The Thirteenth Chapter of the Revelation (London,
                         1656).

p. 338

↑17 godlie   The Logicke of the Most Excellent Philosopher P. Ramus
                         Martyr (London, 1574), p. 13.

p. 339

↓16* memory   William Perkins, "The Art of Prophecying," in Workes
                        (London, 1626-31), II, 645.

↓19* order   Ibid., p. 663.

↑19* premeditated   Ibid., p. 670.

p. 340

↓20 memory   William Chappell, The Preacher, or the Art and
                        Method of Preaching (London, 1656), p. 1; cf. Richard
                        Bernard, The Faithfull Shepherd (London, 1621), p. 159.

↑ 9 speak   Bernard, Faithfull Shepherd, pp. 144-145.

p. 341

↓ 4 men   William Ames, Conscience with the Power and Cases
                        Thereof (London, 1643), bk. IV, p. 76.

↓16 application   Ibid., bk. IV, pp. 76-77.

↑ 7 ambiguity   Bernard, Faithfull Shepherd, p. 252.

p. 342

↓ 1 serveth   Ames, The Marrow of Sacred Divinity (London, 1643),
                        p. 157.

↓10* figures   Perkins, "Art of Prophecying," in Workes, II,
                        654.

↑21 distribution   Bernard, Faithfull Shepherd, p. 216.

p. 342 continued

↑19* doctrines   Perkins, "Art of Prophecying," in <u>Workes</u>, II, 662.

↑16   disposition   Bernard, <u>Faithfull Shepherd</u>, pp. 162-164.

↑ 4   therein   Chappell, <u>The Preacher</u>, p. 18.

p. 343

↓ 5* <u>reclaim</u>   Samuel Willard, <u>Reformation The Great Duty of an Afflicted People</u> (1694), p. 11.

↓15   understandings   Willard, <u>Mercy Magnified on a penitent Prodigal</u> (1684), pp. 3-5.

↑20* incommodious   Thomas Cobbett, <u>A Just Vindication of the Covenant and Church-Estate of Children of Church-Members</u> (London, 1648), p. 131.

↑13   <u>milk</u>   Willard, <u>A Compleat Body of Divinity</u> (1726), p. 32.

p. 344

↓ 5   words   Bernard, <u>Faithfull Shepherd</u>, pp. 40-41.

↓17   conversion   Thomas Hall, <u>Vindiciae Literarum</u> (London, 1655), p. 42.

↓19* God   Perkins, "Art of Prophecying," in <u>Workes</u>, II, 662.

↑16   it   Willard, <u>The Truly Blessed Man</u> (1700), pp. 423-424.

↑ 9   testimonies   Bernard, <u>Faithfull Shepherd</u>, p. 242.

↑ 8   Axiome   Chappell, <u>The Preacher</u>, p. 6.

↑ 1   Argument   <u>Ibid</u>., pp. 13ff.

p. 345

↓17   argument   <u>Ibid</u>., pp. 27-28; cf. Bernard, <u>Faithfull Shepherd</u>, pp. 171-172.

↑18   next   Chappell, <u>The Preacher</u>, p. 30.

p. 346

↓ 6 thing   Bernard, Faithfull Shepherd, pp. 258-263.

↓13 it   Ibid., p. 267.

↓22 hearers   Chappell, The Preacher, p. 123.

↑10 Syllogisme   Bernard, Faithfull Shepherd, pp. 265-271.

↑ 6 laws   Ibid., p. 257.

p. 347

↓ 2 will   Ibid., pp. 272ff.

↓14 dialogue   Ibid., pp. 302-305.

↓22* unteachable   Perkins, "Art of Prophecying," in Workes, II,
                    665-668.

↑10 mind   Chappell, The Preacher, p. 145.

p. 348

↓ 2 businesse   Ibid., p. 153.

↓10 Instruction   Willard, Truly Blessed Man, p. 424.

↓18 operating   Chappell, The Preacher, p. 156.

↑ 8 fast   Ibid., pp. 151-152; cf. Bernard, Faithfull Shepherd,
                    pp. 275-283, 344ff.

↑ 2 impiously   Ames, Conscience, bk. IV, pp. 79-80.

p. 349

↑20 one   Ames, Marrow, pp. A4 recto - A4 verso.

↑17 lost   Ibid., p. 162.

↑14 Gospell   Ibid., p. 160.

↑ 3 minde   Thomas Hooker, A Survey of the Summe of Church-
                    Discipline (London, 1648), p. A4 verso.

p. 350

↓ 5   hid   John Preston, Sinnes Overthrow (London, 1635),
                     p. 104.

↓ 8   perspicacity   Theses rhetoricae, No. 3, 1643; No. 2, 1642.

↓15   blanck   Hooker, The Application of Redemption (London, 1659),
                     p. 194.

↑17   Writings   Increase Mather, Practical Truth's Tending to Promote
                     Holiness in the Hearts & Lives of Christians (1704),
                     p. 2.

↑ 6   Schools   Increase Mather, The Mystery of Christ (1686),
                     Preface.

↑ 2* translated   Perkins, "Art of Prophecying," in Workes, II, 664.

p. 351

↓ 1* ostentation   Ibid., p. 670.

↓ 4   professe   Bernard, Faithfull Shepherd, p. 142.

p. 352

↓ 2   purpose   Bernard, Faithfull Shepherd, p. 108.

↓ 6   vnto   Ibid., pp. 31-34.

↓11   Lamp   Cotton Mather, Just Commemorations (1715), p. 34.

↑11   Auditory   Joshua Moody, Souldiery Spiritualized (Cambridge,
                     1674), p. A2 verso.

p. 353

↓ 6   Oration   Cotton Mather, Just Commemorations, Preface.

↓10   Truth   John Owen, Preface to Increase Mather, Some Important
                     Truths about Conversion (London, 1674).

↓18   Paragraph   Cotton Mather, Selections (ed. Kenneth B. Murdock,
                     New York, 1926), p. 18.

p. 353 continued

↓22 them

Samuel Mather, <u>The Life of the Very Reverend and Learned Cotton Mather . . .</u> (1729), p. 68; cf. Cotton Mather, <u>Parentator</u> (1724), Introduction.

↑ 7 handled

Samuel Sewall, <u>Diary</u>, V Collections of the Massachu-setts Historical Society, v, 119-120.

p. 354

↓ 7 hearers

Cotton Mather, <u>Magnalia Christi Americana</u> (Hartford, 1853-55), I, 311.

↑15 provide
      varnish

Hooker, <u>Survey</u>, pp. a4 verso - b1 recto.

p. 355

↓ 8* entire

[John Norton], <u>A Copy of the Letter Returned by the Ministers of New-England to Mr. John Dury</u> (1664), "Preface to the Reader."

↓22 again

John Saffin, Dedicatory Poem in William Hubbard, <u>A Narrative of the Troubles with the Indians</u> (1677).

↑16 Man

John Cotton, <u>A Brief Exposition Of the whole Book of Canticles</u> (London, 1642), p. 9.

p. 356

↓19 words

Ames, <u>Conscience</u>, bk. IV, p. 78.

↑13 subjects

John Norton, <u>The Heart of N-England rent at the Blasphemies of the Present Generation</u> (Cambridge, 1659), pp. 44-45.

↑11 metaphor

Hooker, <u>The Soules Implantation</u> (London, 1637), p. 207.

p. 357

↑20 Master

Cotton, <u>A Practical Commentary . . . upon The First Epistle Generall of John</u> (London, 1656), p. 242.

p. 357 continued

↑12* increased   Hooker, An Exposition of the Principles of Religion
                      (London, 1645), p. 46.

p. 358

↓ 2 father   Hooker, The Soules Exaltation (London, 1638),
                      pp. 104-105.

↓16* life   Preston, The Cuppe of Blessing (London, 1633),
                      p. 86; cf. Increase Mather, Mystery of Christ,
                      p. 199: "... that we may be able to conceive
                      something of them."

↑19 Inteligible   Cotton Mather, Parentator, p. 215.

↑16 Speaker   Increase Mather, A Call From Heaven To the Present
                      and Succeeding Generations (1679), "To the Reader."

↑ 4* flesh   Perkins, "Art of Prophecying," in Workes, II, 670.

p. 359

↓ 3 duties   Bernard, Faithfull Shepherd, p. 118.

↓ 9 foot   Ames, Marrow, p. A3 verso.

↑20 Divines   Increase Mather, Practical Truth's, p. 2.

p. 360

↓ 4 God   Daniel Gookin, Historical Collections of the Indians
                      in New England, I Collections of the Massachusetts
                      Historical Society, i (1792), 143.

↓10 Generation   Urian Oakes, New-England Pleaded with (Cambridge,
                      1673), p. 23.

↑ 9 sounds   Richardson, Logicians School-Master, p. 12.

↑ 5 others   Ibid., "Rhetorical Notes," p. 69.

p. 361

↓ 4 Alderman   Ibid., p. 70.

p. 361 continued

↓ 9   pollishings   The Bay Psalm Book (Cambridge, 1640), Preface.

↓11* Meeter   Cotton Mather, A Faithful Man, Described and Rewarded (1705), p. 24.

↓14   flies   Jonathan Mitchell, Preface to Michael Wigglesworth, Day of Doom (1701).

p. 362

↓ 2   God   Anne Bradstreet, Works (ed. John Harvard Ellis, Charlestown, 1867), p. 4.

↓14   efficacy   Ames, Marrow, p. A4 verso.

↑ 5* Spirit   Perkins, "Art of Prophecying," in Workes, II, 670.

Chapter XIII: The Covenant of Grace

p.   366

↓ 3* way   Thomas Shepard, Preface to George Phillips, A Reply
                  to a Confutation of some grounds for Infants Baptisme
                  (London, 1645), p. A2 verso.

↓17   trueth   John Norton, The Heart of N-England rent at the
                  Blasphemies of the Present Generation (Cambridge,
                  1659), pp. 26-27.

↑ 3   memory   William Ames, The Marrow of Sacred Divinity (London,
                  1643), p. A3 verso.

p.   368

↓ 6* God   William Perkins, Works, I (London, 1626), p. 21.

↓16   only   Ames, Marrow, p. 110.

↓18   us   Thomas Hooker, The Soules Humiliation (London, 1638),
                  p. 54.

↓22   there   John Preston, Life Eternall (London, 1634), pt. II,
                  pp. 91-92.

↑19   self   John Cotton, A Practical Commentary . . . upon The
                  First Epistle Generall of John (London, 1656), p. 201.

↑ 7   vain   Preston, The Position of John Preston (London, 1654), p.1.

↑ 2   want   Hooker, The Application of Redemption (London, 1659),
                  pp. 299-300.

p.   369

↓ 1   creature   Richard Mather, An Apologie of the Churches in New-
                  England for Church-Covenant (London, 1643), p. 19.

↓ 8   discouragement Hooker, Application of Redemption, p. 300.

↓16   sometimes   Shepard, Works (ed. John A. Albro, Boston, 1853), I, 329.

↓18   Arminianisme Cotton, The Grounds and Ends of the Baptisme of the
                  Children of the Faithfull (London, 1647), p. 17.

p. 369 continued

↑18 himselfe   Cotton, The New Covenant (London, 1654), pp. 48-49; cf.
                       A Treatise of the Covenant of Grace (London, 1671), p. 33.

↑15 Lazarus   Hooker, Application of Redemption, pp. 387-388.

↑12 upon   Ibid., pp. 393, 392.

p. 370

↑10 him   Hooker, The Soules Implantation (London, 1637), pp. 116ff.

↑ 1 God   Ames, Marrow, pp. 131, 117-118; cf. John Ball, A Treatise
                       of Faith (London, 1632), p. 93.

p. 371

↑16 men   Hooker, A Survey of the Summe of Church-Discipline
                       (London, 1648), p. a2 verso.

p. 372

↓16 Age   Samuel Willard, A Compleat Body of Divinity (1726),
                       pp. 754, 31.

↑16 liberty   Shepard, Works, II, 283.

↑ 6 Virgin   William Dell, The Tryal of Spirits (London, 1653), p. 16.

p. 373

↓ 2 Efficient   Willard, Compleat Body, p. 130.

↓ 4 Image   Cotton, The Covenant of Gods free Grace (London, 1645),
                       p. 31.

↓21 bad   Shepard, Works, II, 332.

p. 374

↓ 5* it   Hooker, The Covenant of Grace Opened (London, 1649), p. 27.

↑15 Presidents   Thomas Blake, Vindiciae Foederis (London, 1653), pp. 377, 3

↑ 2 him   Preface to Life Eternall, p. A6 recto.

. 375

11 conditions   Blake, <u>Vindiciae Foederis</u>, p. 3.

20 sincere   Ames, <u>Conscience with the Power and Cases Thereof</u>
                    (London, 1643), bk.V, p. 231.

23 Covenant   Willard, <u>Compleat Body</u>, p. 153.

15* Agents   Willard, <u>The Doctrine of the Covenant of Redemption</u>
                    (1693), p. 68.

 3 other   William Strong, <u>A Discourse of the Two Covenants</u>
                    (London, 1678), p. 241.

. 376

 2* steel   John Ball, <u>A Treatise of the Covenant of Grace</u>
                    (London, 1645), pp. 3-4.

13 all   Blake, <u>Vindiciae Foederis</u>, p. 3.

21* upon   <u>The Covenant Betweene God and Man</u> (London, 1616), p. 29.

13* matter   Ball, <u>A Treatise of the Covenant of Grace</u>, p. 5.

 5 requires   Blake, <u>Vindiciae Foederis</u>, p. 7.

 2 him   Preston, <u>The New Covenant</u> (London, 1629), p. 351.

. 377

 2* him   Willard, <u>Doctrine of the Covenant of Redemption</u>,
                    pp. 115-116.

16 it   Preston, <u>New Covenant</u>, p. 38.

17 faith   Peter Bulkeley, <u>The Gospel-Covenant</u> (London, 1651), p. 80.

 9* condition   Richard Sibbes, <u>Works</u> (ed. Alexander B. Grosart, Edinburgh,
                    1862-64), I, civ.

. 378

 4 covenant   Bulkeley, <u>Gospel-Covenant</u>, p. 133.

<u>p. 378</u> continued

↓ 5 <u>Believer</u>   Joshua Moody, <u>Souldiery Spiritualized</u> (Cambridge, 1674
                  p. 31.

↓ 6* covenant   Thomas Cobbett, <u>A Just Vindication of the Covenant and
                  Church-Estate of Children of Church-Members</u> (London,
                  1648), p. 88.

↓11 another   Cotton, <u>Grounds and Ends of the Baptisme</u>, p. 32.

↓14 referred   Willard, <u>Compleat Body</u>, pp. 152-153.

↓15 Covenant   Bulkeley, <u>Gospel-Covenant</u>, p. 27.

↓21 life   <u>Ibid.</u>, p. 47.

↑17 familiarly Cotton, <u>New Covenant</u>, p. 5.

<u>p. 379</u>

↓11 Decree   Willard, <u>Compleat Body</u>, p. 70.

↓16 them   Norton, <u>A Discussion of that Great Point in Divinity,
                  the Sufferings of Christ</u> (London, 1653), pp. 4-5.

↑16 himself   Hooker, <u>Application of Redemption</u>, p. 337.

<u>p. 380</u>

↓10* justice   John Davenport, <u>The Saints Anchor-Hold</u> (London, 1661),
                  pp. 99-100.

↓12* reigns   Cobbett, <u>Just Vindication</u>, pp. 143-144.

↑20 thee   Preston, <u>New Covenant</u>, p. 316.

↑16 doe   Bulkeley, <u>Gospel-Covenant</u>, p. 276.

↑13 strike   Cotton, <u>The way of Life</u> (London, 1641), p. 415.

↑11 do it   Hooker, <u>The Faithful Covenanter</u> (London, 1644), p. 22.

↑ 7 performance Willard, <u>Covenant-Keeping The Way to Blessedness</u>
                  (1682), pp. 8-9.

p. 381

↓ 6 Covenant   Ibid., p. 52.

↓16 vs   Preston, New Covenant, p. 331.

↑15 too   Increase Mather, Meditations on the Glory of the Lord
                    Jesus Christ (1705), pp. 23-24.

↑13 Curse   Willard, Compleat Body, p. 779.

↑10 faith   Preston, New Covenant, p. 364.

p. 382

↓ 2 Covenant   Shepard, Preface to Bulkeley, Gospel-Covenant,
                    p. Bl recto.

·10 business   Willard, Covenant-Keeping, p. 25.

·18 gathered   Ames, Marrow, p. 170; cf. pp. 170ff; cf. John Ball,
                    A Treatise of the Covenant of Grace, pp. 27ff.

·17 infant   Bulkeley, Gospel-Covenant, pp. 118-119; cf. pp. 166ff.

·12 credence   Hooker, The Saints Dignitie, and Dutie (London, 1651),
                    p. 105.

 4* way   Increase Mather, Preface to Willard, Doctrine of the
                    Covenant of Redemption.

 2* it   Willard, A Brief Discourse of Justification (1686), p. 30.

. 383

 6* Command   Ibid., p. 47.

 9   recompense   Strong, Discourse of the Two Covenants, pp. 1-2.

15* will   Perkins, "The Art of Prophecying," in Workes
                    (London, 1626-31), II, 657.

. 384

22* grace   John Ball, A Treatise of the Covenant of Grace, p. 15.

p. 384 continued

↑16 good   Hooker, <u>Application of Redemption</u>, p. 306.

↑12 it   Cotton, <u>Way of Life</u>, p. 229.

↑ 1 hundreds   Hooker, <u>Soules Humiliation</u>, p. 42.

p. 385

↓ 5 Lord   Cotton, <u>A Treatise of the Covenant of Grace</u>, p. 69.

↓15 Works   <u>Ibid</u>., pp. 33-34.

↑21 promised   Bulkeley, <u>Gospel-Covenant</u>, p. 313.

↑10 <u>Grace</u>   Willard, <u>Morality Not to be Relied on for Life</u> (1700), pp. 20-21.

↑ 1 us   Cotton, <u>Way of Life</u>, p. 206.

p. 386

↓ 2 disobedience   Cotton, <u>New Covenant</u>, p. 126.

↓ 5 repentance   Bulkeley, <u>Gospel-Covenant</u>, p. 83.

↓ 7 vs   Preston, New <u>Covenant</u>, p. 102.

↓13 holiest   Hooker, <u>Saints Dignitie</u>, pp. 4-5.

↓16 it   Willard, <u>Walking with God</u> (1701), p. 17.

↓19 less   Preston, <u>The New Creature</u> (London, 1633), p. 177.

↓22 Corruption   Nehemiah Walter, <u>The Body of Death Anatomized</u> (1707), p. 15.

↑16 Hell   Hooker, <u>Saints Dignitie</u>, p. 117.

↑ 6 corruption   Hooker, "The Poore Doubting Christian," in <u>The Saints Cordials</u> (London, 1629), pp. 352-353.

p. 387

↓ 3 self   Cotton, <u>Covenant of Gods free Grace</u>, p. 12.

p. 387 continued

↓11 Law   Cotton, New Covenant, p. 118.

↑13 life   Bulkeley, Gospel-Covenant, p. 384.

↑11 Mankind   Willard, Covenant-Keeping, p. 33.

↑ 1* sence   John Fry, The Clergy in their Colours (London,
                       1650), pp. 19, 30-31.

p. 388

↓ 7 justification   Bulkeley, Gospel-Covenant, p. 262.

↓12 us   Hooker, Faithful Covenanter, p. 14.

↓14 us   Willard, Compleat Body, p. 782.

↓17* this   Cobbett, Just Vindication, p. 77; cf. Hooker, Faithful
                       Covenanter, p. 12; Bulkeley, Gospel-Covenant, p. 316.

↑21 himselfe   Bulkeley, Gospel-Covenant, p. 315.

↑ 5 doe   Hooker, Faithful Covenanter, pp. 18-19.

p. 389

↓ 2* consent   Sibbes, Works, VI, 8.

↓17 men   Willard, Covenant-Keeping, p. 7.

↑21 salvation   Bulkeley, Gospel-Covenant, p. 323.

↑15* such   Willard, Brief Discourse of Justification, pp. 91-92.

↑11 out   Cotton, Covenant of Gods free Grace, p. 18.

↑ 9 sure   Preston, Life Eternall, pt. II, pp. 84-85.

↑ 6 wrought in us   Bulkeley, Gospel-Covenant, pp. 324-325.

↑ 2 it   Preston, New Creature, p. 23.

p. 390

↓ 3 us   Cotton, <u>Christ the Fountaine of Life</u>, p. 32.

↓ 5 Couenant   Preston, <u>New Covenant</u>, p. 477.

↓ 7 considered   Preston, <u>New Creature</u>, p. 23.

↓21 upon   Bulkeley, <u>Gospel-Covenant</u>, pp. 323-324.

↑11 distribution   Willard, <u>Compleat Body</u>, p. 52.

p. 391

↓ 3 leaven   Bulkeley, <u>Gospel-Covenant</u>, p. 327.

↓ 9 impunity   Shepard, <u>Wine for Gospel Wantons</u> (Cambridge, 1668), p.

↓19 Commandment   Cotton, <u>New Covenant</u>, pp. 134-135.

↓22 grace   <u>Ibid</u>., p. 80.

↑16 business   Jonathan Mitchell, in Shepard, <u>Works</u>, II, 6.

p. 392

↓ 3 otherwise   Norton, <u>Heart of N-England rent</u>, p. 39.

↑10 promiseth   Bulkeley, <u>Gospel-Covenant</u>, p. 383.

p. 393

↓11 man   Shepard, <u>Works</u>, II, 596.

↓16 more   Preston, <u>New Covenant</u>, p. 434.

↑17* it   Willard, <u>Brief Discourse of Justification</u>, pp. 89-90.

↑ 9* him   Hooker, <u>The Unbeleevers Preparing for Christ</u> (London,
                       1638), p. 51.

↑ 6* Iesus   <u>Ibid</u>., p. 58.

↑ 1 Covenant   Preston, <u>Life Eternall</u>, pt. II, p. 83.

p. 394

↓ 9   him   Shepard, Works, II, 31.

↓12   unto   Cotton, A Treatise of the Covenant of Grace, p. 202.

↓18   inexcusable Preston, The Saints Qualification (London, 1633), p. 223.

↓21   meanes   Hooker, "The Poore Doubting Christian," in The Saints
                   Cordials, p. 361.

↑18   commanded   Hooker, Saints Dignitie, p. 83.

↑15* neglect   William Allen, A Discourse of the Nature, Ends, and
                   Difference of the Two Covenants (London, 1673), pp. 26-27.

↑13* it   Willard, Brief Discourse of Justification, p. 130.

↑ 7* Ministery   Phillips, A Reply to a Confutation, p. 15.

↑ 3* Engagements Deodat Lawson, The Duty & Property of a Religious
                   Housholder (1693), p. 12.

↑ 1   God   Increase Mather, Renewal of Covenant the great Duty
                   incumbent on decaying or distressed Churches (1677), p. 4.

p. 395

↓ 5   priviledges Willard, Covenant-Keeping, p. 65.

↓11   escape   Urian Oakes, A Seasonable Discourse (Cambridge, 1682),
                   pp. 19-20.

↑ 1   deny you   Preston, New Creature, p. 31.

p. 396

↓ 3   him   Bulkeley, Gospel-Covenant, pp. 191-192.

↓ 6   grace   Preston, The Saints Daily Exercise (London, 1634), p. 35.

↑ 1   case   William Hubbard, The Happiness of a People in the
                   Wisdome of their Rulers Directing (1676), p. 5.

Chapter XIV: The Social Covenant

p. 401

↓13   death   John Preston, <u>The New Creature</u> (London, 1633), p. 19.

↓17   him   Thomas Hooker, <u>The Saints Dignitie, and Dutie</u>
                    (London, 1651), p. 28.

↓21   sin   Thomas Shepard, <u>Works</u> (ed. John A. Albro, Boston, 1853)
                    I, 344.

↑14   them   Samuel Willard, <u>The Truly Blessed Man</u> (1700), p. 88.

↑ 4* <u>proofs</u>   Richard Baxter, Preface to William Allen, <u>A Discourse</u>
                    <u>of the Nature, Ends, and Difference of the Two</u>
                    <u>Covenants</u> (London, 1673), p. A4 recto.

p. 402

↑ 8   them   William Ames, <u>The Marrow of Sacred Divinity</u>
                    (London, 1643), p. 45.

p. 403

↓ 2* required   William Strong, <u>A Treatise Shewing the Subordination</u>
                    <u>of the Will of Man unto the Will of God</u> (1657), p. 37.

↓ 8   Law   Hooker, <u>The Saints Guide</u> (London, 1645), pp. 10-11.

↓16   Rational   Willard, <u>A Compleat Body of Divinity</u> (1726), p. 807.

↑ 4   accomplishment Cf. Shepard, Preface to Peter Bulkeley, <u>The Gospel-</u>
                    <u>Covenant</u> (London, 1651), p. B2 verso.

p. 404

↓12   man   Jonathan Russell, <u>A Plea for the Righteousness of God</u>
                    (1704), pp. 6-7.

↑20   men   Willard, <u>The Barren Fig Trees Doom</u> (1691), p. 42.

↑11   Reprobation John Cotton, <u>The Way of Congregational Churches</u>
                    <u>Cleared</u> (London, 1648), pt. I, p. 33.

p. 406

5* parson   Willard, The Doctrine of the Covenant of Redemption
                   (1693), p. 41.

10* pleas'd   Milton, Paradise Lost, bk. III, 11.238-241.

21 beleevers   Charles Chauncy, The Plain Doctrin of the Justification
                   of a Sinner in the sight of God (London, 1659),
                   pp. 139-140.

16* Men   Willard, Doctrine of the Covenant of Redemption, pp. 5ff.

5* law   Ibid., pp. 96-97.

1 iniquitie   Hooker, Saints Dignitie, p. 33.

p. 407

12* Faith   Willard, Doctrine of the Covenant of Redemption, p. 3.

15* sent   Ibid., pp. 26-27.

p. 408

18 consent   The Hutchinson Papers (A Collection of Original Papers
                   Relative to the History of the Colony of Massachusetts-
                   Bay) (The Prince Society, Albany, 1865), I, 79-80.

16 impiety   Robert C. Winthrop, Life and Letters of John Winthrop
                   (Boston, 1869), II, 440.

11 duties   Hooker, A Survey of the Summe of Church-Discipline
                   (London, 1648), pt. I, p. 70.

p. 409

1 duties   Ibid., pt. I, p. 69.

12 not   Ibid., pt. I, p. 50.

7 done   Cotton, An Exposition upon The Thirteenth Chapter of
                   the Revelation (London, 1656), pp. 72, 77.

p. 410

↓ 7 Patern   John Norton, <u>Three Choice and Profitable Sermons Upon</u>
                   <u>Severall Texts of Scripture</u> (Cambridge, 1664), p. 35.

↓ 9* woe   Thomas Shepard, Jr., <u>Eye-Salve</u> (Cambridge, 1673), p. 28

↓11 Rule   Willard, <u>Compleat Body</u>, pp. 149-150; cf. p. 565;
                   pp. 620 (sig. Eeee4 verso) ff.

↓16* welfare   Jonathan Mitchell, <u>Nehemiah on the Wall in Troublesom</u>
                   <u>Times</u> (Cambridge, 1671), p. 7.

↓18* good   <u>Ibid</u>., p. 12.

↑15 defence   Cotton, <u>An Exposition upon The Thirteenth Chapter of</u>
                   <u>the Revelation</u>, pp. 109, 111-112.

↑ 6* Principles   Mitchell, <u>Nehemiah on the Wall</u>, pp. 11-12.

p. 413

↓17 will   Cotton, <u>Christ the Fountaine of Life</u> (London, 1651),
                   pp. 34-35.

↓21* it   Hooker, <u>The Christians Two Chiefe Lessons</u> (London,
                   1640), p. 10.

↑15 faithfulnesse Bulkeley, <u>Gospel-Covenant</u>, pp. 345-346.

p. 415

↓20 them   Richard Mather, <u>An Apologie of the Churches in New-</u>
                   <u>England for Church-Covenant</u> (London, 1643), p. 8;
                   cf. J. W. Gough, <u>The Social Contract</u> (Oxford, 1936),
                   pp. 26-27.

↑17 1630   <u>Gods Promise to His Plantation</u> (London, 1630).

↑16* 1633   <u>The Danger of Desertion</u> (London, 1641).

↑15 1630   <u>The Winthrop Papers</u> (Massachusetts Historical Society,
                   Boston, 1929-31), II, 282-295.

↑15 1637   <u>Hutchinson Papers</u>, I, 79-113.

p. 415 continued

↑13 Court   John Winthrop, Winthrop's Journal, "History of New
                    England," 1630-1649 (ed. J. K. Hosmer, New York, 1908),
                    II, 237-239.

p. 416

↑18 man   Winthrop Papers, II, 293-294.

↑16 Solitariness   Cotton, A Briefe Exposition with Practicall Observa-
                    tions upon The Whole Book of Ecclesiastes (London,
                    1654), p. 85.

↑14 family   Hutchinson Papers, I, 81.

↑10 paine   Winthrop Papers, II, 288.

↑ 4 Man   Ibid., II, 283.

p. 417

↓14 self   Willard, Compleat Body, p. 619 (sig. Eeee4 recto).

↓16 nature   William Strong, A Discourse of the Two Covenants
                    (London, 1678), p. 8.

↓22* disband   Henry Gibbs, The Right Method of Safety (1704),
                    pp. 10-11.

↑ 4 abolished   Joseph Easterbrooks, Abraham the Passenger his
                    Privilege and Duty (1705), p. 20.

p. 418

↓ 6 them   Shepard, "Election Sermon, in 1638," in New England
                    Historical and Genealogical Register, XXIV (1870), 363.

p. 419

↓12 unity   Winthrop Papers, II, 290-291.

↑17 thitherward   William Adams, The Necessity of the Pouring Out of the
                    Spirit from on high (1679), p. 14.

p. 419 continued

↑ 3 man   Norton, The Heart of N-England rent at the Blasphemies
                    of the Present Generation (Cambridge, 1659), p. 32.

p. 420

↓ 8 pleases   Roger Williams, The Bloudy Tenant, of Persecution, for
                    cause of Conscience, discussed ([London?], 1644), p. 140.

↓14 him   Hooker, The Faithful Covenanter (London, 1644), pp. 10-11

↓15 himself   Bulkeley, Gospel-Covenant, p. A2 verso.

↑18 regiment   Ibid., pp. 219-220.

↑14 Society   John Eliot, The Christian Commonwealth, III Collections
                    of the Massachusetts Historical Society, ix, 143.

↑10 Lawes   Cotton, A Brief Exposition Of the whole Book of
                    Canticles (London, 1642), p. 44.

↑ 9 Common-wealth Cotton, The New Covenant (London, 1654), p. 34.

p. 421

↑17 another   John Davenport, "A Sermon Preach'd at The Election of
                    the Governour at Boston in New-England, May 19th, 1669,"
                    pp. 4-6, in Publications of the Colonial Society of
                    Massachusetts, X (1907).

p. 422

↓ 3 ecclesiasti-   Winthrop Papers, II, 293.
     call

↓14 spirit   Winthrop's Journal (ed. J. K. Hosmer), II, 118.

↓19 representative Ibid., II, 240.

↓23 God   Ibid., II, 86-87.

↑ 1 estate   Ibid., II, 83.

p. 423

↓14 magistrates   Robert C. Winthrop, Life and Letters of John Winthrop,
                   II, 435.

↑21 Commonalty   Cotton, A Briefe Exposition . . . of Ecclesiastes, p. 220.

↑20 Covenant   Cotton, The Way of the Churches of Christ in New-England
                   (London, 1645), p. 4.

↑17 commonwealth Thomas Hutchinson, The History of the Colony and
                   Province of Massachusetts-Bay (ed. Lawrence Shaw Mayo,
                   Cambridge, 1936), I, 415.

p. 425

↓ 9* Rom. 13.5   The Laws and Liberties of Massachusetts. Reprinted from
                   . . . the 1648 edition . . . (ed. Max Farrand, Cambridge,
                   1929), Preface.

↑ 9 covenant   Winthrop's Journal (ed. J. K. Hosmer), II, 237-239.

p. 427

↓21 Gospel   Norton, Three Choice and Profitable Sermons, p. 7.

↓22* commandments Thomas Shepard, Jr., Eve-Salve, p. 50.

↑ 1 will   Bulkeley, Gospel-Covenant, p. 346.

p. 428

↓12 herein   Shepard, Works, III, 346.

↓15 good   Ibid., III, 348.

p. 429

↓ 7 confusion   William Hubbard, The Happiness of a People in the
                   Wisdome of their Rulers Directing (1676), pp. 8-10.

p. 431

↓ 2* sake   The Colonial Laws of Massachusetts. Reprinted from
                   the Edition of 1660 (ed. William R. Whitmore, Boston,
                   1889), p. 120.

Chapter XV: The Church Covenant

↓21 Worship   William Hubbard, The Benefit of a Well-Ordered
                    Conversation (1684), p. 99.

↑16 over   Vindiciae Clavium [attributed to Daniel Cawdrey]
                    (London, 1645), p. A1 recto.

↑10* thereof   In Cotton Mather, Elijah's Mantle (1722), pp. 3-4.

p. 434

↑16 them   John Cotton, The Way of the Churches of Christ in
                    New-England (London, 1645), p. 84.

p. 435

↑18 another   Richard Mather, Church-Government and Church-Covenant
                    Discussed (London, 1643), pp. 13-14.

↑ 8 therof   Richard Mather, An Apologie of the Churches in New-
                    England for Church-Covenant (London, 1643), p. 3.

p. 436

↓ 8 conjoyned   Ibid., p. 5.

↓13 justly   Thomas Hooker, A Survey of the Summe of Church-Discipline
                    (London, 1648), pt. I, p. 204.

↓17 refuseth   Cotton, Way of the Churches of Christ, p. 57.

↓21* ends   John Davenport and William Hooke, A Catechisme
                    (London, 1659), p. 28.

↑10 true Church   Samuel Hudson, The Essence and Unitie of the Church
                    Catholike Visible (London, 1645), p. 40.

↑ 5* covenants   Thomas Shepard and John Allin, A Defense of the Answer
                    made unto the Nine Questions or Positions sent from
                    New-England, Against the Reply Thereto by . . . Mr.
                    John Ball (London, 1648), p. 73.

p. 437

↓11 inventions   Cotton, Way of the Churches of Christ, p. 65.

p. 437 continued

↓21 reasoning   Samuel Willard, A Compleat Body of Divinity (1726),
                      p. 613 (sig.*Iii4 recto).

↑ 7 Anglicans   Hudson, A Vindication of the Essence and Unity of the
                      Church Catholike Visible (London, 1650), p. 19;
                      Davenport, The Power of Congregational Churches
                      Asserted and Vindicated (London, 1672), p. 7.

p. 438

↓11 New   Richard Mather, Apologie, pp. 8-9.

↑13 another   Cotton, Way of the Churches of Christ, pp. 61-62.

p. 439

↓ 7 Aristotelians   Hudson, A Vindication of the Essence, p. 77.

↓12* studies   Hudson, An Addition or Postscript to the Vindication
                      of the Essence and Unity of the Church-Catholick
                      visible . . . (London, 1658), p. 2.

p. 440

↓12 us   Cotton, Of the Holinesse of Church-Members (London,
                      1650), p. 30.

p. 441

↓14 parallel   Hudson, A Vindication of the Essence, pp. 152-153.

↓19 Table   Samuel Rutherford, A Survey of the Survey of that
                      Summe of Church-Discipline Penned by Mr. Thomas
                      Hooker . . . (London, 1658), p. 99.

↑20 no   Hudson, A Vindication of the Essence, p. 96.

↑ 4 soules   Cotton, The Bloudy Tenent, Washed, And made white
                      in the bloud of the Lambe (London, 1647), pp. 67-68.

p. 442

↓12 Faith   William Ames, The Marrow of Sacred Divinity (London,
                      1643), p. 140.

p. **442** continued

↓15 essence   Ibid., pp. 137-138.

↓19 Church   Cotton, The Way of Congregational Churches Cleared (London, 1648), pt. II, p. 11.

↑15 visible   Hudson, A Vindication of the Essence, p. 18.

↑14 Donatism   Rutherford, A Survey of the Survey, pp. 12, 39-40, 519.

p. **443**

↑22 Church   Cotton, Of the Holinesse of Church-Members, p. 87.

↑13 Jesus   Cotton, Way of the Churches of Christ, p. 2.

p. **444**

↓ 3 men   Cotton, The Keys of the Kingdom of Heaven (London, 1644), p. 2.

p. **445**

↓ 4* Lord   Thomas Cobbett, A Just Vindication of the Covenant and Church-Estate of Children of Church-Members (London, 1648), p. 137.

↓ 6 purity   Cotton, The way of Life (London, 1641), p. 357.

↓11 Servants   Increase Mather, Renewal of Covenant the great Duty incumbent on decaying or distressed Churches (1677), p.

↓17 Ordinances   Cotton, Way of the Churches of Christ, p. 2.

↑16 Law   Richard Mather, Apologie, p. 7.

↑ 1 politie   Samuel Stone, A Congregational Church is a Catholike Visible Church (London, 1652), pp. G2 verso - G3 recto.

p. **446**

↓ 4 estate   Richard Mather, Apologie, p. 26.

p. 446 continued

↓ 7   relation   Davenport, <u>The Power of Congregational Churches
                      Asserted and Vindicated</u>, pp. 41-42.

↑19   opposition   William Rathband, <u>A Briefe Narration of some Church
                      Courses Held in Opinion and Practise in the Churches
                      lately erected in New England</u> (London, 1644),
                      pp. 13-15, 20.

p. 447

↓ 2   churchmen   Hooker, <u>Survey</u>, pt. I, p. 70.

↓ 4   Covenant   <u>Ibid</u>., pt. 1, p. 78.

↓ 8   Church   <u>Ibid</u>., pt. III, p. 24.

↑13   thereof   Richard Mather, <u>Apologie</u>, pp. 2-3.

↑ 9* Church-way   Cobbett, <u>Just Vindication</u>, p. 16.

↑ 4   love   Cotton, <u>The Covenant of Gods free Grace</u> (London, 1645),
                      p. 22.

p. 448

↓19* covenant   Shepard and Allin, <u>A Defense of the Answer</u>, p. 106.

↑12   Covenant   Richard Mather, <u>Apologie</u>, pp. 12-13.

↑ 5   Common-wealth   Cotton, <u>Way of the Churches of Christ</u>, p. 4.

↑ 2   Church   Davenport, <u>The Power of Congregational Churches
                      Asserted and Vindicated</u>, p. 37.

p. 449

↓ 3   compact   Richard Mather, <u>Apologie</u>, pp. 21-22.

↓10   receive   Daniel Cawdrey, <u>The Inconsistencie of the Independent
                      Way</u> (London, 1651), pp. 98-101.

↑16   Church-Cove-   Cotton, <u>Way of the Churches of Christ</u>, pp. 63-64.
      nant

p. 449 continued

↑13 accordingly   Rutherford, A Survey of the Survey, p. 153.

↑ 8 thereof   Richard Mather, Apologie, p. 16.

p. 450

↓ 1 it   Quoted in Cotton Mather, Magnalia Christi Americana
                     (Hartford, 1853-55), I, 553.

↓ 7 Gospel   Increase Mather, Renewal of Covenant, p. A2 verso.

↑12 Latine   Rutherford, A Survey of the Survey, p. 274.

↑ 8 Mistress   Rathband, A Briefe Narration, pp. 25-26.

p. 451

↓ 4 commanded   Richard Mather, Church-Government and Church-
                     Covenant Discussed, p. 66.

↓10 alteration   Davenport, The Power of Congregational Churches
                     Asserted and Vindicated, pp. 129-130.

↓15 themselves   Richard Mather, Church-Government and Church-
                     Covenant Discussed, p. 47.

↑18 Scripture   Ibid., p. 42.

↑16 Churches   Ibid., pp. 47-48.

↑ 5* Band   Shepard and Allin, A Defense of the Answer,
                     pp. 130-131.

↑ 3 Christ   Richard Mather, Church-Government and Church-
                     Covenant Discussed, p. 60.

p. 452

↓ 7 commanded   Ibid., p. 59.

↓11 Church   Cotton, Way of the Churches of Christ, p. 100.

↓14 Democracy   Cotton Mather, Magnalia, I, 437.

p. 452 continued

↑12 Christ   John Eliot, <u>The Christian Commonwealth</u>, III <u>Collections of the Massachusetts Historical Society</u>, ix, 144.

↑11 God   Richard Mather, <u>Church-Government and Church-Covenant Discussed</u>, p. 38.

↑ 5* charity   Hooker, <u>The Covenant of Grace Opened</u> (London, 1649), p. 19.

p. 453

↓16 partialities   Rathband, <u>A Briefe Narration</u>, pp. 8-9.

↑19 member   Richard Mather, <u>Apologie</u>, p. 21.

p. 454

↓18 slaves   Thomas Lechford, <u>Plain Dealing; or Newes from New England</u> [London, 1642] (ed. J. Hammond Trumbull, Boston, 1867), pp. 151, 89.

↑15 English   <u>The Hutchinson Papers (A Collection of Original Papers Relative to the History of the Colony of Massachusetts-Bay)</u> (The Prince Society, Albany, 1865), I, 214-223.

p. 456

↑ 8 church   Richard Mather, <u>Apologie</u>, p. 17.

↑ 1 Church   Richard Mather, <u>Church-Government and Church-Covenant Discussed</u>, p. 11.

p. 457

↓ 6 priviledges   <u>Ibid</u>., p. 21.

↓11 doubted   Cotton, <u>A Discourse about Civil Government in a New Plantation Whose Design is Religion</u> (Cambridge, 1663; attributed to John Davenport), p. 21.

↓12 it   Cotton, <u>Of the Holinesse of Church-Members</u>, pp. 29-30.

p. 457 continued

↓18   off   Shepard, Works (ed. John A. Albro, Boston, 1853),
                         III, 324.

↑10   God   Cotton, Keys of the Kingdom of Heaven, p. 50.

↑ 4* God   Cobbett, The Civil Magistrates Power In matters of
                         Religion Modestly Debated . . . (London, 1653),
                         pp. 66-67.

p. 458

↑15   end   Shepard, Works, III, 288-289.

↑ 2   Christ   Hooker, Survey, pt. II, pp. 79-80.

p. 459

↓ 2   privileges   Cobbett, Civil Magistrates Power, p. 25.

↓ 7   examples   Cotton, A Brief Exposition Of the whole Book of
                         Canticles (London, 1642), p. 22.

↓12   gods   Cotton, The Result of a Synod at Cambridge in
                         New-England (London, 1654), p. 6.

↑20   forced   Hooker, Survey, pt. III, p. 3.

p. 460

↓ 2   sake   Cotton, Way of Life, pp. 386-387.

↓20* discretion   Joseph Sedgwick, Learning's Necessity to an Able
                         Minister of the Gospel (London, 1653), p. 42.

↑19   work   Hooker, Survey, pt. I, p. 1.

↑11   establishment   Richard Mather, Apologie, p. 9.

↑ 9   us   Cotton, Way of the Churches of Christ, pp. 26-27.

p. 461

↓ 2 together   Thomas Edwards, <u>Reasons against the Independent
                       Government of Particular Congregations</u> (London,
                       1641), pp. 11-13.

↓20 Thucydides   Davenport, <u>The Power of Congregational Churches
                       Asserted and Vindicated</u>, p. 123.

p. 462

↑ 1 enjoyed   Willard, <u>Compleat Body</u>, p. 635 (sig.Gggg4 recto).

Chapter XVI: God's Controversy with New England

p. 463

↓ 9   Angels   Increase Mather, Angelographia (1696), pp. 36-37.

↑ 4   execution   Increase Mather, The Doctrine of Divine Providence
                      (1684), p. 51.

p. 464

↑ 7   both   Nicholas Noyes, New-Englands Duty and Interest, To be
                      an Habitation of Justice, and Mountain of Holiness
                      (1698), p. 43.

↑ 5* arriv'd   Cotton Mather, A Midnight Cry (1692), pp. 30-32.

p. 465

↓10   causes   John Cotton, A Briefe Exposition with Practicall
                      Observations upon the Whole Book of Ecclesiastes
                      (London, 1654), pp. 21, 129-132.

↓22   God   Ibid., p. 131.

↑11   deservings   Thomas Hooker, A Survey of the Summe of Church-
                      Discipline (London, 1648), p. A2 recto.

p. 466

↓ 6   truth   James Allen, New-Englands choicest Blessing
                      (1679), p. 11.

↑20   Attempt   Urian Oakes, The Soveraign Efficacy of Divine
                      Providence (1682), p. 13.

p. 467

↓10   correctly   Cotton, The Way of the Churches of Christ in
                      New-England (London, 1645), p. 28.

↓14   Writers   Cotton, A Practical Commentary . . . upon The First
                      Epistle Generall of John (London, 1656), pp. 77-78.

↓17   ages   Cotton, A Brief Exposition Of the whole Book of
                      Canticles (London, 1642), p. 165.

↓20   Literature   Cotton Mather, Eleutheria (London, 1698), pp. 7-9.

p. 467 continued

↑17   Atheisme   Cotton, A Practical Commentary . . . upon The First
                        Epistle Generall of John, p. 174.

↑ 8   Truth   Cotton, The Way of Congregational Churches Cleared
                        (London, 1648), pt. I, p. 24.

↑ 6   Lions   Cotton, A Brief Exposition Of the whole Book of
                        Canticles, p. 154.

p. 468

↓ 2   resurrection   Cotton, A Brief Exposition Of the whole Book of
                        Canticles, p. 158.

↓ 3   reform   Cotton, An Exposition upon The Thirteenth Chapter
                        of the Revelation (London, 1656), p. 106; Hooker,
                        Survey, p. A4 recto.

↓ 5   Spirit   John Davenport, The Power of Congregational Churches
                        Asserted and Vindicated (London, 1672), p. 87.

↓ 7   Ministry   Cotton, A Brief Exposition Of the whole Book of
                        Canticles, p. 161.

↓14   England   Cotton, Way of Congregational Churches Cleared,
                        pt. I, p. 31.

↓21   Christ   Cotton Mather, Eleutheria, pp. 35-38.

p. 469

↓ 1   Christ   Cotton, An Exposition upon The Thirteenth Chapter
                        of the Revlation, pp. 260-261.

↓ 7   Popery   Cotton, The Churches Resurrection (London, 1642),
                        pp. 18-19.

↓16   tryall   John Preston, Life Eternall (London, 1634), pt. I,
                        p. 87.

↓18   Puritans   Hooker, The Soules Implantation (London, 1637), p. 104;
                        The Soules Preparation for Christ (London, 1638), p. 13.

↑18   England   Hooker, The Danger of Desertion (London, 1641), pp. 5-6.

p. 469 continued

↑ 7 Expected   Increase Mather, Ichabod (1702), p. 80.

↑ 2 us   Cotton, An Exposition upon The Thirteenth Chapter
                 of the Revelation, pp. 260-261.

p. 470

↑16 sword   Ibid., pp. 241-242.

↑10 alone   Peter Bulkeley, The Gospel-Covenant (London, 1651),
                 pp. 431-432.

↑ 7 Righteousness Davenport, "A Sermon Preach'd at The Election of the
                 Governour at Boston in New-England, May 19th, 1669,"
                 p. 15, in Publications of the Colonial Society of
                 Massachusetts, X (1907).

↑ 3* people   Thomas Shepard and John Allin, A Defense of the Answer
                 made unto the Nine Questions or Positions sent from
                 New-England, Against the Reply Thereto by . . . Mr.
                 John Ball (London, 1648), p. 7.

p. 471

↓ 9 fore-Fathers Cotton, An Exposition upon The Thirteenth Chapter
                 of the Revelation, p. 77.

↓12 simplicity Cotton, Churches Resurrection, p. 20.

↓14 Apostles   Cotton, An Exposition upon The Thirteenth Chapter
                 of the Revelation, p. 262.

↓17 together   Cotton, A Discourse about Civil Government in a New
                 Plantation Whose Design is Religion (Cambridge, 1663;
                 attributed to John Davenport), pp. 18-19.

↓18 dream   Thomas Shepard, "Election Sermon, in 1638," in New
                 England Historical and Genealogical Register, XXIV
                 (1870), 363.

↑21 Commonwealth William Hubbard, The Benefit of a Well-Ordered
                 Conversation (1684), pp. 95-96.

↑16 time   Hooker, Survey, p. al recto.

p. 471 continued

↑ 8   congregations   Cotton, <u>The way of Life</u> (London, 1641), p. 185.

↑ 2   duties   Cotton, <u>The New Covenant</u> (London, 1654), pp. 166, 139.

p. 472

↑15   excess   Michael Wigglesworth, "God's Controversy with New-England," in I <u>Proceedings of the Massachusetts Historical Society</u>, xii (1873), 88.

↑11   there   Joshua Moody, <u>Souldiery Spiritualized</u> (Cambridge, 1674), p. 26.

↑ 6   time   Increase Mather, <u>Practical Truths tending to promote the Power of Godliness</u> (1682), p. 184.

↑ 4   Plantations   Increase Mather, Preface to Samuel Torrey, <u>A Plea For the Life of Dying Religion from the Word of the Lord</u> (1683), p. A2 recto.

p. 473

↓12   granted   Shepard, <u>Works</u> (ed. John A. Albro, Boston, 1853), II, 65, 375.

↓16   things   Cotton, <u>A Briefe Exposition . . . of Ecclesiastes</u>, p. 1.

↓21   Lord   Cotton, <u>Way of Life</u>, p. 413.

↑11*   godliness   James Fitch, <u>An Explanation of the Solemn Advice</u> (1683), p. 45.

↑ 8   upward   Urian Oakes, <u>New-England Pleaded with</u> (Cambridge, 1673), p. 33.

↑ 5   God   Samuel Willard, <u>Mercy Magnified on a penitent Prodigal</u> (1684), p. 27.

↑ 2   Creature   Eleazer Mather, <u>A Serious Exhortation to the Present and Succeeding Generation in New-England</u> (2 ed., 1678), p. 9.

p. 474

↓16   paradeis   Wigglesworth, "God's Controversy with New-England," p. 87.

p. 475

↑20 in   John Danforth, <u>The Vile Prophanations of Prosperity</u>
                        (1704), p. 12.

↑17* be   Peter Folger, <u>A Looking Glass for the Times</u> (Rhode
                        Island Historical Tracts No. 16, Providence, 1883), p. 17

p. 476

↓ 1 Saints   Cotton, <u>The Grounds and Ends of the Baptisme of the</u>
                        <u>Children of the Faithfull</u> (London, 1647), p. 161.

↓ 4 God   Hooker, <u>The Faithful Covenanter</u> (London, 1644), p. 4.

↓21* Englanders   Cf. Preston, <u>The Golden Scepter held forth to the</u>
                        <u>humble</u> (London, 1638), pp. 12-13.

↑14 Commandements   Hooker, <u>Faithful Covenanter</u>, p. 19.

p. 477

↑ 4 it   <u>The Winthrop Papers</u> (Massachusetts Historical Society,
                        Boston, 1929-31), II, 293-295.

p. 478

↑12 ensew   Wigglesworth, "God's Controversy with New-England," p. 88

↑ 4 disobedience   Willard, <u>Useful Instructions for a professing People</u>
                        (Cambridge, 1673), p. 11.

p. 479

↓ 2* Threatnings   Willard, <u>Rules for the Discerning of the Present Times</u>
                        (1693), p. 24.

↓13 Providences   Willard, <u>Mercy Magnified</u>, pp. 53-54; cf. Joseph Rowlandso
                        <u>The Possibility of Gods Forsaking a People</u> [1682]
                        (Somers Tracts, London, 1812), VIII, 584-585.

p. 480

↓ 5* people   Willard, <u>Rules for the Discerning</u>, pp. 24-25.

p. 480 continued

↓15   same   William Stoughton, New-Englands True Interest; Not to Lie (Cambridge, 1670), pp. 10-11.

↓21   stand   Willard, Israel's True Safety (1704), p. 8.

↑18   room   Increase Mather, A Discourse Concerning the Danger of Apostacy (2 ed., 1685), p. 61.

↑ 5   appears   John Rogers, A Sermon Preached before His Excellency the Governour (1706), pp. 30-31.

p. 481

↓ 1   them   Willard, A Sermon Preached Upon Ezekiel 22 (1679), p. 3.

↓11   Heaven   John Ball, A Treatise of Faith (London, 1632), p. 363.

↓13   him   Cotton, Way of Life, p. 454.

↑18   wayes   Ball, A Treatise of Faith, pp. 63-64.

↑12   to it   Willard, A Compleat Body of Divinity (1726), p. 709.

↑ 4   them   Hooker, Faithful Covenanter, p. 7.

p. 482

↓ 5* Allegiance   Willard, Reformation The Great Duty of an Afflicted People (1694), p. 36.

↓10   cause   Willard, The Peril of the Times Displayed (1700), p. 74.

↓16   are   Ibid., p. 73.

↑10   us   Jonathan Russell, A Plea for the Righteousness of God (1704), p. 9.

↑ 3   Repentance   Willard, "The only sure way to prevent threatned calamity," in The Child's Portion (1684), p. 175.

p. 483

↑16   irresistible   Shepard, Works, III, 312.

p. 483 continued

↑12 us   Hooker, <u>Faithful Covenanter</u>, p. 11.

p. 484

↓ 5 Heaven   Grindal Rawson, <u>The Necessity of a Speedy and Thorough</u>
                       <u>Reformation</u> (1709), pp. 9-10.

↓18* it   Willard, <u>Rules for the Discerning</u>, p. 24.

p. 488

↓ 8 appears   Urian Oakes, <u>Soveraign Efficacy</u>, pp. 18-19.

↓16 God   Willard, <u>Love's Pedigree</u> (1700), p. 17.

↓20 will   Hooker, <u>The Soules Vocation</u> (London, 1638), pp. 312-313

↑14 no   Cotton, <u>Grounds and Ends of the Baptisme</u>, p. 64.

↑ 5 <u>him</u>   Hooker, <u>The Application of Redemption</u> (London, 1659),
                       p. 299.

p. 489

↓10 hurt   Willard, <u>Israel's True Safety</u>, p. 10.

↓20 Judicial   Willard, <u>Covenant-Keeping The Way to Blessedness</u>
                       (1682), p. 66.

Acknowledgments

To the Reverend Paul T. Gerrard, who resembles the Puritans in being both a Calvinist and a humanist, I owe my earliest interest in many of the ideas about which Miller wrote. Had it not been for the outstanding Latin teaching of Miss Dorothy Cameron, I could not have checked many of Miller's notes against the original sources. Kenneth Lynn introduced me to Miller's work when I was a graduate student and gave an earlier draft of the introduction a most helpful reading. Daniel Aaron, Norman Fiering, and David Hollinger also provided support and encouragement at various stages of this project, but I alone am responsible for the opinions expressed in the introduction. Elizabeth Miller generously answered my questions about the circumstances in which both volumes of *The New England Mind* were published. The notes to *The Seventeenth Century* are published here with her permission and that of Houghton Library. Martha Shaw and Tom Noonan, successive curators at Houghton Library, and other members of the staff there courteously and cheerfully brought me the hundreds of volumes I requested. The Babson College Board of Research, chaired by Edward Handler, paid for typing. Janet Manter and Concetta Stumpf, of the college word-processing center, skillfully and patiently prepared the typescript. Carol Hoopes improved the introduction with a rather critical reading of it, but she was in all other ways forbearing to her usual, unusual degree.